Retirement Planning and Taxes for Canadians

What Bankers Know,
and YOU Should Know Too — About . . .

Retirement Planning and Taxes for Canadians

OLIVER
PUBLISHING

Retirement Planning and Taxes for Canadians

September 2008

ISBN 978-1-894749-68-8

Publisher: R. Dale Oliver
Writer: Susan Yates
Editor: Patricia Kennedy
Technical Editor: Alexander Duncan
Editorial Assistance: Fernanda de Melo
Cover Design: Kitty McKechnie www.kmckecknie.com
Text & Design and Layout: Computer Composition of Canada

Oliver Publishing
151 Bloor Street West, Suite 800
Toronto, Canada M5S 1S4
Tel: (416) 922-9604 Fax : (416) 922-5126
Toll Free 1-800-238-0377
e-mail: info@oliverpublishing.ca
www.oliverpublishing.ca

Printed and bound in Canada

Table of Contents

Introduction

What Your Banker Knows

The Qualifications

When you go in to meet a financial advisor at your local bank branch, you are likely meeting an employee of one of the largest companies in Canada—with all the money, power, and prestige behind them that comes from occupying that lauded space in the Canadian economy. In 2007, over 255,000 employees in Canada worked for Canadian banks, and they were paid over $20.5 billion in salaries and benefits.

The scope of knowledge needed by financial advisors at the banks is truly impressive—not just about financial planning, which of course encompasses retirement planning, but also about investments and mortgages. Bank-based advisors are well and thoroughly trained on a variety of subjects on an on-going basis, and they are encouraged to complete courses from the Canadian Bankers Association, such as the Personal Financial Planning™ Course. Some will also have their Certified Financial Planner™ designation, an internationally recognized standard of expertise in financial planning. This benefits you the consumer, plus you have the peace of mind that comes from dealing with a salaried, non-commissioned, or non-fee-based employee.

Expertise

As it currently stands, your bank-based advisor can provide you with access to many financial products—savings accounts, Guaranteed Investment Certificates, mutual funds, bonds, and Treasury bills; stocks are sold through their affiliates. They cannot sell life insurance, other than "mortgage" insurance, although the banking industry is lobbying heavily to change that. If that change takes place, you will see life insurance operations set up with, but separate from, the bank branches.

Importance to Retirement Planning

Because of their training and the overview they have of the entirety of your finances, bankers have unique perspective on the process of retirement planning.

About Retirement and Taxes

This book is going to show you what bankers learn about retirement planning and how they practise what they know.

Some of the questions we'll ask and answer in these pages include:

- Can I afford to retire?
- How do I estimate my retirement income?
- How much will I receive from the government?
- What type of company benefit plan offers the best pension?
- What should I do when my RRSP matures?
- How can I protect myself from inflation?
- What taxation issues will affect me when I retire?

With some careful planning, your retirement can be everything you imagined.

A Question of Timing

As this book is being completed in September 2008, a financial crisis threatens our economy, and you may well feel that your retirement plans have been demolished. Remember that retirement can last for decades; this crisis will pass just as others have before. This is a very important time to study the information presented in this book, so you will better understand your options. Being prepared for change is a good strategy, no matter where you stand in respect to your retirement plans.

Chapter 1

What You Need to Know about Retirement Planning

It's the last moments of the job that has been your life. You've got a big fat pension from your employer, a totally topped-up RRSP, your mortgage is paid off, you have no debts, the kids are settled, and you and your spouse are in perfect health, ready to spend the next 28.3 years travelling, working on your hobbies, and living life to the fullest—at which point you will peacefully die in your sleep. You're ready to shake hands with your colleagues and move into retirement.

This scenario may be the one you dream of as you think of retirement, but in reality it is far from the truth for those who face retirement or have retired. Let's look at some of the facts about retirement . . .

Some Retirement Realities

A recent study carried out by Ipsos-Reid showed that 42% of Canadians retired with credit-card debt. It also showed that 33% of Canadians have debt during retirement, and that the average debt load is $35,000.

That big pension most employees anticipate receiving is failing to materialize, as employers have moved towards implementing defined-contribution pensions, in which the value of the pension is a result of your own investment savvy.

Perfect health can be a blessing and a curse; you can easily now outlive your money, because you simply failed to take into consideration your increased life expectancy. You can face great, continuing, and escalating expenses for assisted home care or nursing-home care.

And—this might surprise you—don't count on spending your time puttering in the garden or jetting off to Tuscany: another survey has indicated that more than half of pre-retirees expect to be working at least part-time during retirement. There is now a significant amount of research pointing to the need people have to work post-retirement, not for financial but psychological reasons.

A recent survey indicated that 33% of Canadian retirees were still working or were self-employed.

All this points to a retirement that may be quite different from that you imagined—not necessarily worse, but certainly different. The facts illustrate that retirement planning is not just about the cash in the bank—though let's not understate its importance! Retirement planning should encompass the goals and needs you will face in retirement, and this includes not only your need for cash but also for the lifestyle choices you will make.

When to Retire

There are five ways you can retire (or not):

- through early or forced retirement;
- on the arrival of the "normal"retirement age;
- on a staggered, or transitional, basis;
- late;
- never.

Early and Forced Retirement

The decision about when to retire may be one that is not entirely within your control; you may be offered an early retirement package. Packages often look very attractive, and turn out to be less so when you take the time to consider what is being offered and what early retirement can mean to you.

It is not unusual for such packages to be very complicated, and taking the time to discuss their details with your banker or financial advisor who has expertise in personal financial planning will be time well spent.

Here are some things you should consider:

Can You Afford To Retire?

Receiving a "package" might just be the exit you are looking for if you have achieved financial independence. However, you need to become aware of how early retirement might affect your pension plan.

> Lots of people think they want to receive "the package" from their employer; it is essential to understand what that package really delivers in the way of financial security.

What Are the Tax Consequences?

If you are offered a lump sum, can it be transferred tax free into your RRSP, or will it be locked-in? If your RRSP is already topped up, must you take the lump sum into income? This could result in a considerable tax bill that will eat into the value of the amount offered in the package.

If funds are locked in, for instance in a Locked-in Retirement Account or LIRA, there are restrictions on the maximum amount that can be withdrawn each year, unlike the case with an RRSP or RRIF.

What Benefits Will You Lose?

If you are covered by your employer for a medical plan that includes prescription drugs, dental care, vision care, or other medical coverage, you will need to know whether this plan might continue until your normal retirement age or whether these benefits will cease when you accept the package you have been offered.

What Happens If You Say "No"?

Is there a chance the package is being offered in the place of outright termination? If so, can you afford to say no? On the other hand, will your rejection of the offer put you in a position in which you might be transferred to another job or another location with reduced pay?

Do You Want To Retire?

This is where the non-financial factors come into play. Do you want to leave your job? Are you ready to disengage from corporate culture: the people, the structure, perhaps the travel you do in your job? Many who are offered a package fail to consider this factor adequately, because the cash that is offered simply seems too tempting to resist.

EARLY RETIREMENT AND GOVERNMENT BENEFITS

You can begin receiving your Canada Pension Plan/Quebec Pension Plan retirement pension as early as age 60. The pension is reduced by 0.5% for each month you are younger than 65; thus if you started it at age 60, the amount you receive will be reduced by 30% from the amount you would receive at age 65.

To receive CPP between the ages 60 and 64, you must have either stopped working or have earned less than the current monthly maximum CPP benefit ($884.58 in 2008) in the month your pension begins and the month prior. You can then return to receiving your full income, though you will no longer be making CPP payments.

Normal Retirement

The normal age for retirement is considered to be age 65. If you have a registered pension plan with your employer, the Normal Retirement Date is the date at which the pension will commence, according to the terms of the plan. Usually this is when the member turns 65, but it may be some other age, such as 62.

If you are a member of a pension plan and retire before this date, you will receive a reduced pension. Retiring ten years early will usually pay about half the full pension, because the pension has to be paid out for a longer time based on fewer contributions made. Some pension plans permit early retirement when the sum of your age and contributions reach a certain level.

At age 65 you will be entitled to receive your full CPP/QPP monthly retirement pension. Old Age Security also begins at age 65, as does the Guaranteed Income Supplement for those who pass an income test.

The age of 70 was selected in the early twentieth century as the age of eligibility for a government pension, when life expectancy was about 60.

In Canada there is no mandatory retirement age, except when there is a direct correlation between age and qualifications for specific jobs relating to strength and endurance, such as police work. (Nova Scotia does have mandatory retirement, which will end on July 1, 2009.)

Transitional Retirement

Transitional, or phased, retirement is a relatively new concept that acknowledges that a person may not be psychologically prepared to move from the full-blown work environment to the full-blown non-work environment. It is a way to ease into retirement that can begin when you are satisfied that you can afford to retire and your employer is prepared to have you work less than the regular work week.

Transitioning provides the key benefit of allowing you to accumulate more savings, while adjusting to reduced income. Instead of learning how to make changes or implementing changes overnight, as you must in the traditional retirement model, you have a chance to practise cutting back on what you spend to match it up to what you allot to living expenses. You may learn that you need to develop some cash-management skills, such as budgeting, that you have not had to use for many years.

There are several transitional methods. One sees you take a sabbatical of, for instance, one month's duration every year over a period of perhaps five years leading up to the intended retirement date to give you a chance to practise retirement. Perhaps you start taking off a week a month, or one month every three. Transitioning can start slowly and build as time passes until full retirement simply arrives one day, without the impact that it might otherwise have had.

Another option is part-time work with your employer, or part-time work in an entirely new job. This is also a time when you could take the opportunity of exploring self-employment by becoming a "consultant" or taking on another position in which you set the schedule to suit your needs.

Transitioning into retirement can reveal an important gap in your retirement planning: what are you going to do with the extra time? While men are more likely than women to have extra time on their hands during retirement, the majority of retirees do not report having excess time to fill. The challenge is to find a way to fill the time that is meaningful for you. Whether that is through volunteer work, paid work, spending more time with family, or whatever you choose, it is universally agreed that you must engage in some activity to provide a context in which "retirement" can occur. In other words, if you watch TV all day because you enjoy watching TV after work, you will soon find that watching TV really isn't that fulfilling. Full-time leisure time can soon become more of a chore than working ever was.

Late Retirement

As CPP/QPP benefits go, retirement after age 65 reverses the pattern of the early retiree. In late retirement, your benefits *increase* by 0.5% per month to age 70, at which point there are no further increases. This means that, if you retire at age 68, your benefits will increase by 18% (0.5 x 12 x 3).

If you continue to work after the normal retirement age, you may find that your income reduces your OAS benefits, and in fact, all those who earn more than $64,718 in 2008 will start to see their OAS benefits reduced. Those with a net income of $104,903 in 2008 are subject to a full clawback, in which all their OAS benefits must be repaid to the federal government.

Never Retired

Staying involved in productive activities is critical to aging successfully. While it is not common for employees to continue to work without ever retiring, it is not unusual for business owners to work in some capacity into their eighties.

For people who have devoted so much energy and time to the success of their businesses, retirement can be synonymous with "end of life." These folks are definitely well served by transitioning into retirement so they can find the new meaning and new direction their lives can take.

Getting Ready for the Big Day

Many employers offer counselling services for employees preparing to retire. Subjects that can be covered include: health care, financial planning, housing arrangements, life adjustments, legal issues, organizing leisure time, and using skills for a second career. If your employer offers such a program, take advantage of it. If you have to go it alone without the benefit of employer-provided counselling, you may find local courses devoted to some or all of these subjects. The local library or Canada Employment Centre are good resources to check.

You should also bring in expert help and consult with your banker, financial advisor, lawyer, and accountant on the help each can provide. Completing this research can be like a job in itself, and perhaps a good way to begin your retirement. Regardless of how you go about it, preparation is key to adjusting happily to this new phase of your life.

Chapter 2

Calculations Used in Retirement Planning

There are few things more important than the numbers when it comes to retirement planning; so many questions revolve around "how much," such as, how much should I be saving? What will my savings grow to in ten years? How much do I need in my RRSP? The following is an exercise in liberation for you. If you master these few steps with a financial calculator, you no longer need to wonder, guess, or rely on others to give you the numbers you need. You can do them yourself; and you can monitor your progress and update as you go, for numbers will change during the period you are saving for retirement.

Here are some of the calculations you will be able to perform with a financial calculator:

- how much an investment, paying compound interest, will be worth at the end of a period of time (known as the time value of money);
- how much should be invested today to yield a specified amount in the future (known as the present value of money);
- how much your savings will be worth at a point in the future (known as the future value of money);
- how much is needed upon retirement to yield a specific income (known as an annuity payment);
- how much needs to be saved to yield a specific income received at the beginning of the year and the end of the year (known as the present value of an annuity).

The following steps for these calculations are based on using a Hewlett-Packard 10BII calculator, which is widely available through Grand & Toy or Staples stores; it is very similar to the Sharpe calculator. You should check the manual that will accompany your financial calculator to ensure it functions in the same way as the instructions below indicate.

All calculators and the calculations important to you are based on five functions:

- n for the number of periods or payments to be invested
- i for the interest rate over the period
- PV for present value
- PMT for payment amount
- FV for future value.

Using an HP10BII calculator

Make sure when you press the gold (or orange) shift button and then *"clear all,"* 1 P_YR comes up on the display. This means you are in the 1-payment-per-year mode. If any other number comes up, e.g., 12, you are in the 12-payments-per-year or monthly-payment mode, and your answers will not correspond to ours.

To get in the 1-payment-per-year mode:

- Press 1
- Press the gold shift button and then press the P/YR button in the top row of buttons. P/YR is on the PMT button. 1 will display on your screen.
- Press the shift button and then the Clear All button. 1 P_YR will display.*

Beginning and Ending Modes

Most calculations are done in the "ending mode." There is no display on the screen showing ending mode. Some calculations, such as having annuity payments paid at the beginning of the year, require the calculator to be in the "beginning mode."

To set the beginning mode, press the gold (or orange) shift button and then the BEG/END button that is at the end on the second row and on the MAR button. The word "BEGIN" is displayed on the screen.

To switch back to the "ending mode," simply press the gold (or orange) shift button and then the BEG/END button. The word "BEGIN" disappears from the screen.

***Note:** In the calculation examples that follow throughout the book, the execution of these initial steps to clear the calculator prior to the execution of the example calculation is assumed. Also, any keystroke not specifically mentioned (e.g., PMT) is assumed to be zero.

Getting Down to Business

Now let's see how you can use this calculator to give you the information you need. Follow each step as shown. For instance, in the calculation below, in Step 1 you will key in 50,000, press the PV key, and your display will show -50,000. Next, Step 2, you will key 4, press the i key, and your display will show 4. In Step 3, you key in 5, press the n key, and your display will show 5. Finally, in Step 4 you will press the FV key, and your display will show 60,832.65.

Value of an Investment with Compound Interest

You deposit $50,000 into a bank account that pays 4% annually. If you leave the interest payments in the account, how much will you have in the account after five years?

Step	Key	Press	Display will show
1	50,000(+/-)	PV	-50,000
2	4	I	4
3	5	N	5
4		FV	60,832.65

You will have $60,832.65 in the account after five years.

Investment Needed to Yield an Amount in the Future

If you wanted to have $50,000 in five years, how much would you have to deposit today in an account that paid 4% annually?

Step	Key	Press	Display will show
1	50,000(+/-)	FV	-50,000
2	4	I	4
3	5	N	5
4		PV	41,096.36

You would have to deposit $41,096.36 in the account today to have $50,000 in five years.

The Value of Savings

You deposit $4,500 into your RRSP every year for the next 20 years. If the savings grow at an annual rate of 9.5%, how much will you have then? (Deposits are made at the beginning of each year.)

Make sure calculator is in "ending mode."

Step	Key	Press	Display will show
1	4,500(+/-)	PMT	-4,500
2	20	N	20
3	9.5	I	9.5
4		FV	243,550.05

You will have $243,550.05 in 20 years.

Amount Needed to Yield a Specified Income

You want to have your savings funded so that you will receive an annual income of $45,000 for the following 30 years. You assume your investments can achieve a return of 11%. The payments will be made at the end of each year.

Make sure calculator is in "ending mode"

Step	Key	Press	Display will show
1	45,000(+/-)	PMT	-45,000
2	30	N	30
3	11	I	11
4		PV	391,220.67

You must have $391,220.67 saved to yield an annual income of $45,000 for 30 years.

If, however, you want to receive the income at the beginning of the year, your calculator needs to be in "beginning mode."

Step	Key	Press	Display will show
1	45,000(+/-)	PMT	-45,000
2	30	N	30
3	11	I	11
4		PV	434,254.94

You must have $434,254.94 in your RRIF. More funds are needed because you are reducing the amount that compounds growth by taking the money out at the beginning of the year.

Make It Work for You

Now you can plug in all the variables, such as amounts, periods of time, and presumed rates of return to develop numbers personalized to you and your needs.

Chapter 3

The Process of Retirement Planning and Government and Pension Income

Those financial planners with an interest in retirement planning, such as your banker, will agree there is a logical sequence of steps in the development of a retirement plan. These steps provide an interesting overview for any person who is retiring to be aware of. They form a process that you can follow whether you plan on your own or with expert help.

The process of retirement planning identifies your goals and objectives to ensure adequate funding will be in place when it is needed. This process includes:

- establishing retirement goals and objectives;
- determining your current financial status;
- estimating your retirement income;
- making a projection of how much money you will need to retire;
- establishing an investment plan to meet retirement needs.

Developing the Plan

Retirement Goals and Objectives

A retirement goal leads to a retirement objective. How so? A goal is simply an idea of what you want to do—for instance, retire at age 90. The objective is the amount of money you need to turn the goal into reality, let's say $500,000. Another goal common among Canadian retirees is to live in a warmer climate for part of the winter; the objective then would be to have approximately $180,000 available to purchase a retirement home at the date of retirement and $20,000 available per year to pay the expenses for that home. Another way of approaching that goal would be for the retiree to consider renting instead of buying; in that case, the objective would be to have $266,841.30 available upon retirement to pay for 15 years of renting, for six months a year, at $4,000 per month, assuming 49% annual rate of return. You can use the present value of an annuity to make this calculation yourself. Note that the present value is less than the sum of the withdrawals, because the balance is earning interest over the period.

Thus, your goals must be identified before your objectives. They will drive your saving and investing during the pre-retirement phase, so that your objectives can be met. This is something only you can do, in consultation with your spouse. You will need to discuss how you see your future lifestyle and how you will spend all the extra time that is now yours.

> The Canadian Bankers Association reports that, post-retirement, you will have an extra 2,000 hours of free time every year.

Your Current Financial Status

You need a complete financial snapshot of where you are in order to determine where you are going. (The worksheets at the end of the book will help you with this task.)

To do this you need to gather:

- bank statements of cash accounts;
- bank statements of savings and money-market investments;
- any loan agreements;
- mortgage papers;
- statements of stock, bond, mutual fund, and other investments;
- insurance policies, including your life insurance, health insurance, property insurance, and statement of group benefits in the group-membership booklet you would have received from your employer if you are enrolled in a group plan;
- any other financial commitments you have, such as education for your children.

A money-market investment is a short-term debt instrument, including certificates of deposit, commercial paper, bankers' acceptances, T-bills, and certain types of discount note.

The point of pulling all this information together is to prepare a net worth statement. Net worth is the amount by which your assets exceed your liabilities.

Your assets will be listed at their fair market value. They include your home, other properties you own for personal use, investments, and the value of life insurance. Liabilities are all those obligations you have, such as a mortgage and loans.

Fair market value is the price you would get for selling an asset on the open market.

In addition, to ensure you have taken all financial obligations into consideration, you will need to review:

- copies of your income-tax filings for the last three years;
- your will; and
- your separation agreement and divorce decree (if relevant).

By deducting your liabilities from your assets, you will find your net worth—a key indicator of your financial health. Your net worth statement should be prepared annually, preferably at the same time each year, to see where you stand and whether there is a change in the figure. Subtle changes may occur over the course of a year that you will not be aware of until you do the net worth calculation. An increase shows you are increasing assets faster than they are being depleted; a decrease can be cause for concern and may require you to analyze not only why your net worth has dropped but what steps you need to take to reverse the decline.

Sources of Retirement Income

Most people rely on three sources for their retirement income:

- government benefits;
- a pension from their employer;
- personal savings and investments (to be discussed in the following chapter).

Government Benefits

Canadian government retirement pensions include:

- Old Age Security (OAS);
- the Guaranteed Income Supplement (GIS);
- the Allowance;
- the Canada Pension Plan/Quebec Pension Plan (CPP/QPP).

Canadian government pensions are administered by Human Resources and Skills Development Canada (see www.hrsdc.gc.ca).

Old Age Security (OAS)

The ***Old Age Security*** (**OAS**) pension is a monthly benefit payable to all Canadians or legal residents, age 65 and over, who apply for the benefit and meet residency requirements. The benefits are adjusted quarterly and are indexed to the Consumer Price Index (CPI), which means they are adjusted for inflation. Benefits received from the OAS are taxable income.

Please contact Human Resources and Skill Development Canada or consult its website to learn about residency requirements.

An application for OAS pension benefits can be made six months prior to eligibility, and must include your proof of age and legal residence status. Payments begin the month after the month you meet the requirements, but may be made retroactively for up to 12 months if the application is late.

You are entitled to receive payments while absent from Canada if you lived in Canada for a total of 20 years after age 18. If you have fewer than 20 years of residence, you can receive payments outside of Canada for a maximum of six months. However, if you then return to Canada, payments will begin again in the month of your return.

OAS Clawback

Those who earn high incomes during retirement—perhaps as a combination of income from private pension plans, registered plans, investments, and the Canada Pension Plan/Quebec Pension Plan—will have their OAS benefits taxed through a special tax known as the clawback, which reduces the amount of pension received. It is possible to have your entire OAS pension taxed back to the government. The partial clawback begins at $63,511; the entire clawback kicks in at $103,100.

Guaranteed Income Supplement (GIS)

The Guaranteed Income Supplement (GIS) is a monthly benefit paid to you if you are a resident of Canada who receives Old Age Security and has little other income. You must be 65 or older and pass an annual income test.

You cannot plan to receive the GIS; you will receive it only as an emergency measure that will top you up to where you would be if you lived on welfare payments.

The GIS is paid differently for single pensioners and for married pensioners. The amount a single pensioner receives is reduced by $1 for each $2 of other monthly income; the amount a married pensioner receives is reduced by $1 for each $4 of the couple's other combined monthly incomes. More details on GIS rates and the Allowance (see below) can be acquired from Human Resources and Skills Development Canada.

You must reapply annually for the GIS. Benefits are not taxed and will continue to be paid if you leave Canada for up to a maximum of six months.

The Allowance

The Allowance, formerly called the Spouse's Allowance, is a monthly benefit paid to you if you are a resident of Canada whose legal or common-law spouse receives Old Age Security and the Guaranteed Income Supplement, and has little other income. You must be between 60 and 64 and meet residency and income-needs criteria.

Canada Pension Plan/Quebec Pension Plan (CPP/QPP)

The Canada Pension Plan (CPP) and Quebec Pension Plan (QPP) have virtually the same requirements and benefits, and for this reason are frequently discussed as if they are one plan. The distinction is that the CPP applies to all Canadians outside the province of Quebec; the QPP is for Quebec residents only.

The CPP is available as a retirement pension, as a disability pension, and as survivor benefits. It is important to remember that you must apply to receive your pension; it does not start automatically. It is generally recommended that the application be made six months prior to starting to receive CPP.

The CPP disability pension is available to those younger than age 65 who are able to prove a severe and prolonged disability.

The following concepts are fundamental to understanding the CPP retirement pension:

- your contributions;
- the year's basic exemption (YBE);
- the year's maximum pensionable earnings (YMPE);
- your pensionable earnings;
- your average monthly pensionable earnings (AMPE).

Contributions to the CPP are made by both you and your employer, unless you are self-employed. Both you and your employer contribute 4.95% for a total of 9.9% (in 2008) of your employment earnings between a minimum and maximum amount. You cannot make additional contributions.

If you are self-employed, you are responsible for the entire contribution (9.9%). However you receive a tax break for the portion of the contribution that represents the employer's share (4.95%). This amount can be deducted from taxable income, and your share is allowed a 15.25% federal tax credit.

Contributions are made by all those who work, beginning at age 18, including part-time employees. Contributions end either when you begin receiving the pension, at age 70 (if you have not already begun to receive it), or if you die.

CPP contributions kick in after you have earned $3,500. This is called the *year's basic exemption* (YBE). In other words, no contributions are made for the first $3,500 of income. Conversely, CPP contributions are not made on amounts you earn over $44,900. This is called the year's *maximum pensionable earnings* (YMPE).

It is the amount between this minimum and maximum on which your contribution is based; this is called your pensionable earnings. Therefore, if you earn more than $44,900, your pensionable earnings will be $41,400 ($44,900 - $3,500). But if you earned, let's say, $30,000, your pensionable earnings would be $26,500 ($30,000 - $3,500).

Your *average monthly pensionable earnings* (AMPE) is used to determine the amount of your monthly retirement pension. It is your total pensionable earnings divided by the number of months that you contributed (or 120 months, whichever is greater). Your monthly retirement pension at age 65 is 25% of the AMPE to a maximum. The maximum CPP pension in 2008 was $884.58.

Another way to look at this is:

a) Determine Total Pensionable Earnings:

All pensionable earnings together = total pensionable earnings

b) Determine Average Monthly Pensionable Earnings

The greater of: $\frac{\text{Total Pensionable Earnings}}{\text{No. of Months of Contributions}}$ = Average Monthly Pensionable Earnings

or 120 months (whichever is greater)

c) Determine Monthly CPP Retirement Pension

Average Monthly Pensionable Earnings x 25% = Monthly Retirement Pensions

Early or Late CPP Retirement Options

As we have already discussed, you can receive the CPP as young as age 60, or delay it to a later age. Benefits, however, are capped at age 70.

CPP Death Benefit

As a CPP contributor, you will receive a death benefit payable to your estate. The benefit is equal to the total payment that you would have received for six months at age 65. The maximum death benefit is $2,500.

CPP Pension Sharing (also discussed in the last chapter)

If you have contributed to CPP, and both you and your spouse or common-law partner are at least 60 years old, you can share your CPP pension. This is called an assignment.

The assignment of CPP redistributes income from one person to another; the amount of pension is not increased or decreased by assignment. The benefit of doing so is to move income to your spouse who is in a lower tax bracket and thus pay less tax on what you receive. An assignment will end if you divorce, if your non-contributor spouse becomes a contributor, if either you or your spouse die, or one year after you separate.

In the case of marriage breakdown, whether legal or common-law, you and your spouse can divide pensionable earnings equally. The application must be made within three years of the date of marriage breakdown.

After a CPP contributor dies, the spouse may apply for a surviving spouse's pension, whether the spouse is legal or common-law. The amount the surviving spouse will receive depends on how long contributions were made to the plan, his or her age when the contributor dies, whether he or she is receiving a CPP pension, if he or she is disabled, and if there are dependent children.

Employer Pensions

Employers have a variety of means by which they can provide retirement income to their employees:

- Registered Pension Plans;
- Deferred Profit-sharing Plans;
- Group Retirement Savings Plans;
- Individual Pension Plans;
- Retirement Compensation Arrangements;
- Supplemental Executive Retirement Plans (SERPs).

Registered Pension Plans

Registered Pension Plans (RPPs) are the most common of all employer-sponsored pension savings plans.

However, there is a great deal of misconception about these plans. For instance, in 2001, half of all full-time permanent employees in the private sector reported having a group Retirement Savings Plan or Registered Pension Plan. In fact, 8% of them, approximately 390,000 people, had no such coverage.

Further, many of those covered by RPPs fail to understand their benefits and the type of pension they and their survivors will receive.

RPPs are trusts registered by your employer with the Canada Revenue Agency. The plan must comply with regulations in the *Income Tax Act* that specify the maximum amount that may be contributed to the plan.

Your employer will contribute to the plan and you may be required or permitted to make additional contributions. The contribution you make to your pension plan will be deducted from your contribution limit to your Registered Retirement Savings

Plan, thereby preventing "double-dipping" when it comes to tax deductions on contributions.

Your contribution to your pension plan must be made by December 31 in the year a deduction is claimed in order to be tax deductible.

You have until 60 days after the end of the calendar year to make an RRSP deduction.

There are two types of defined pension plans. You may be enrolled in either:

- a defined-benefit plan, or
- a defined-contribution plan (also called a money-purchase plan).

Funds contributed to these plans are "locked in." Locking-in means that money cannot be withdrawn before retirement, and at retirement it provides a pension with a yearly cap. If you leave an employer and have one of these plans, the funds will roll over to another locked-in account until you reach retirement age.

Locking-in does not mean the funds must remain with the firm that sponsored the plan if you do not continue to be employed by that firm.

On retirement, the funds from either of these plans will be received as a pension, or they can be used to purchase a life annuity, be transferred to a Locked-in Registered Retirement Plan (also called a Locked-in Retirement Account or LIRA), or transferred to a Life Income Fund (LIF). The annuity, LIRA, and LIF will all provide you with an annual income.

Defined-Benefit Plans (DBPs)

If you have a defined-benefit plan you will know exactly how much you will receive when you have retired. Hence, the benefit can be taken into account accurately as a source of income during retirement. There is no investment risk to the employee with a DBP. The retirement benefit does not depend on market performance.

The amount of pension received from a defined-benefit plan will be calculated based on the type of plan in which you have been enrolled. There are four:

- the career-average earnings plan;
- the final-average earnings plan;
- the best-earnings plan;
- the flat-benefit plan.

The ***career-average earnings plan*** records a pension credit in every year of employment.

You contribute a fixed percentage of your earnings, and your employer contributes the amount needed to raise the fund to a level sufficient to provide the total pension credit for that year. Since an employee typically earns less when he or she first joins a firm, the amount of pension will be decreased by the lower-income years because of the averaging effect.

In a ***final-average earnings plan,*** the final income-earning years (usually the highest income-earning years) are used as the basis for determining the pension income.

A ***best-earnings plan*** bases pension benefits on an average of the best years of pensionable earnings, usually three or five consecutive years.

A ***flat-benefit plan*** specifies the age and the number of years of service that are required before you are eligible for the benefit. A formula is typically used that specifies the amount of pension "earned" each year, and this is multiplied by the number of years of employment.

Defined-Benefit Plans: Best Bet for Highest Pension		
$$$$	largest pension....	best-earning plan
$$$	next largest....	final-average plan
$$	then	career-average plan
$	lowest pension....	flat-benefit plan

Opting out of a DBP

If you leave the company with vested benefits, the Commuted Value of the defined-benefit plan can be transferred to a locked-in plan, such as a locked-in Registered Retirement Savings Plan or another registered pension plan, or can be used to purchase an annuity. The Commuted Value, or Transfer Value, is a lump-sum payment. The basis for calculating the value is dictated by the Canadian Institute of Actuaries.

Your benefits are usually considered vested after you have worked for your employer for two years. At that point you are entitled to the contributions your employer made to the plan.

The Commuted Value is calculated as the present value of the pension benefit earned to date. The present value is tied to the yield on the Government of Canada long-term bond. These interest rates are established every month. The Commuted Value will be higher when interest rates are low and lower when interest rates are high.

After your money has been transferred from the DBP, your employer no longer has an obligation to you for your retirement income.

VESTED BENEFITS

If you terminate your employment before you are vested, you are only entitled to your contributions with interest, up to the termination date of employment. The minimum period in which vesting can occur is two years.

If you have not made contributions, your benefit is zero. If you are vested, however, you are entitled to transfer the pension as discussed above or to a deferred pension, payable at the Normal Retirement Date.

Defined-Contribution Plans (DCPs)

Whereas with a defined benefit plan you know what to expect, you will not know how much pension you will receive with a defined-contribution plan. This is because contributions are made, and then interest rates and investment earnings affect the total value of the funds that have been contributed.

With a defined-contribution plan, you will have a choice of investments to which your money can be directed. These investments are the same investments available to the self-directed RRSP plan holder, and include stocks, bonds, mutual funds, and mortgage-backed securities (MBS), amongst others, though your employer will choose which investments will be offered. Usually the range of investments is quite limited.

Defined-contribution plans are becoming more popular with employers, because the employer is off the hook for providing a specified amount of pension; the amount of pension is a result of how you invest the contributions you make. Many employees fail to take advantage of the investment opportunities with which they are provided, and simply default to the money-market option as an investment vehicle. This choice may provide an unwelcome surprise to the retiree when he or she receives a pension that is much smaller than was expected.

A money-market fund is the most conservative type of mutual fund, in which net returns are equal to, or even slightly less than, a savings account, due to fees charged by the fund company.

If you are a member of a defined-contribution plan, you must be involved in the investment of the contributions to ensure they are correctly allocated for your retirement objectives, your risk tolerance, and your age.

The Pensions Paid by Defined Plans

All employees enrolled in an RPP receive an annual pension statement. This statement is frequently misinterpreted by the employee, who can be mistaken about what will be paid and when. It is important to analyze the statement with your financial advisor or plan administrator at work to understand how much you will receive—and when.

The pension statement will show the amount of pension earned as of the statement date and payable at the Normal Retirement Date. As we have seen, the Normal Retirement Date is the date when the pension will begin, according to the terms of the plan document. This is usually age 65.

The amount shown will be the pension that is payable, either on an annual or a monthly basis. Be sure to understand the payment mode to avoid any confusion.

Often the statement will show the amount of pension that will be earned from the date of the statement to the Normal Retirement Date, based on assumptions about future earnings and assuming you remain in the plan until the Normal Retirement Date. The pension earned to the date of the statement, plus the pension to be earned, gives a conservative estimate of what your pension might be at the Normal Retirement Date.

The **maximum** yearly pension that can be provided by a defined-benefit plan is the lesser of:

- $2,333, multiplied by the number of years of pensionable service;

or

- 2% per year of pensionable service, multiplied by the average of the best consecutive years of remuneration. Typically, three or five consecutive years is the period used (e.g., monthly pension = 1.5% x average monthly earnings of last 5 years x years of service).

Remember, there is no minimum or maximum to the pension provided by the defined-contribution plan.

You must choose between several forms of pension.

The Normal Form of Pension

The Normal Form of Pension is typically a single life pension with a guaranteed period of income based only on your life, so you will receive an income for as long as you live. The pension statement should indicate the Normal Form of Pension that will be paid to you at the Normal Retirement Date.

A guaranteed number of payments will be received under this form of pension, regardless of when death occurs. For example, if your plan provides a life-only pension with a 5-year guarantee, and you received 22 monthly payments prior to your death, your beneficiary will be paid a lump sum totalling 38 payments (60 – 22).

A Joint-and-Last-Survivor Pension

Regulations in many jurisdictions require that, if you are married, you must take a Joint-and-Last-Survivor pension, unless your spouse specifically declines that option in writing when the pension benefit is chosen.

The amount of your pension will be reduced if you take a Joint-and-Last-Survivor pension, when the Normal Form is a life-only pension, with or without a guaranteed period. The reduction occurs because, while the joint pension is less than the single life, it is expected to be paid for a longer period of time. The younger your spouse is, the larger is the reduction. There is a reduction even if your spouse is older than you are. This is because a unit of two people is more likely to live longer than one individual of the same age. The amount of the reduction can vary by plan and option chosen.

Typical pension options are Single Life guaranteed 5 years, Single Life guaranteed 10 years, Single Life guaranteed 15 years, Joint-and-Last-Survivor, reducing to 60% on member death, Joint-and-Last-Survivor, reducing to 75% on member death, and Joint-and-Last-Survivor, continuing at 100% on the member's death. Other options are possible.

The following example illustrates how the pension is reduced for the various forms. It assumes the retiring pension-plan member is a male aged 65, and the Normal Form is a Single Life guaranteed 5 years of $25,750 per year.

	Pension Amount	**Reduction**
Normal Form Single Life guaranteed 5 years	$25,750	
Single Life guaranteed 10 years	$24,850	3%
Single Life guaranteed 15 years	$23,560	9%
Joint-and-Last-Survivor 60%, Female Spouse Age 62	$23,150	10%
Joint-and-Last-Survivor 60%, Female Spouse Age 68	$24,000	7%
Joint-and-Last-Survivor 100%, Female Spouse Age 62	$21,560	16%
Joint-and-Last-Survivor 100%, Female Spouse Age 68	$22,800	11%
Joint-and-Last-Survivor 60%, Female Spouse Age 40	$20,600	20%

Bridge Benefits

Some plans will pay you a bridge benefit from retirement until the age when your government pensions begin. The benefit may be a flat dollar amount or it may be tied to CPP and/or OAS benefits.

The amount of benefit will be shown on your pension statement if it is provided by the pension plan.

Cost-of-Living Adjustment (COLA)

About 20% of the Defined Benefit Plans in Canada provide for an automatic Cost of Living Adjustment (COLA). If the COLA is automatic, the statement will inform you how the adjustment is to be applied. Without a COLA, over your retirement you will see a loss of purchasing power that results from creeping inflation.

Some COLAs do not apply unless the Consumer Price Index exceeds a certain minimum level, such as 3%. In this situation, you will not receive a COLA in those years in which the CPI is less than 3%.

The Consumer Price Index (CPI), published by Statistics Canada, measures the increase in the cost of living.

Alternatively, your employer may increase pensions at irregular intervals when the company feels the purchasing power of the pensions has been eroded. These are called ad hoc increases. Your pension statement will be silent on this point, because it is not guaranteed.

Marriage Breakdown

The rules governing the splitting of pension credits in the event of the breakdown of a marriage or common-law relationship vary by jurisdiction. An official document decreeing the division of the pension assets must be provided to the plan administrator in order for division to take effect.

Death Benefits

If you die before beginning to receive your monthly retirement benefit, and you were not vested—in other words, if you are not entitled to the contributions your employer made to the plan because you were enrolled in the pension plan with the employer for less than two years before your death—the value of your plan will consist of your contributions with interest, to the date of death. If you made no contributions, the value of the plan may be zero.

If you were vested, your spouse or beneficiaries will be entitled to the commuted value or Transfer Value of the pension as of the date of your death. Some plans permit your spouse to convert the Transfer Value to a monthly pension of equal value. The value of the plan can roll over tax-free to your spouse's Locked-in Retirement Account (LIRA), if he or she is less than 71. A LIRA was previously known as a Locked-in RRSP. The LIRA is established with the institution of his or her choice. Because it is locked-in, the funds can only be withdrawn for retirement purposes.

A Transfer Value is the amount of an immediate lump-sum payment that is estimated to be equal in value to the future pension payments the member can expect at Normal Retirement. The basis for calculating the Transfer Value is dictated by the Canadian Institute of Actuaries. The interest rates, which are based upon long-term bond rates, are established every month.

Your spouse may also roll over the pension to an annuity.

Death Prior to Retirement: Defined-Contribution Plan

As with the Defined-Benefit Plan, the value of your plan is partly a function of whether you and your employer contributed to the plan; if you are not vested, you do not receive the employer contribution, and your spouse receives your contributions plus interest. This is called the Account Value.

The Account Value can be received by a spouse or beneficiary on a tax-free basis when it is rolled into a LIRA.

Death After Retirement: Defined-Benefit Plan

The amount to be received by your spouse will be the result of the form of pension you selected with your employer and the provisions of the plan.

Death After Retirement: Defined-Contribution Plan

Your spouse will receive the Account Value, just as he or she would have done if your death occurred before retirement. The same restrictions apply on the funds.

Taxation of Defined Plans

You are not taxed on your employer's contribution to a defined plan as an employee benefit, but you are taxed on the pension income when it is received.

Some plans permit you to make additional contributions; these additional payments can be deducted for tax purposes in the year in which they are contributed, although, as previously noted, they will reduce your RRSP contribution room.

When you begin to receive pension income, it is taxed as regular income, although up to $2,000 per year may be exempted by the pension income credit.

Deferred Profit-sharing Plans (DPSPs)

Like defined plans, a Deferred Profit-sharing Plan (DPSP) is a trust created for all employees of a company, or for one or more classes of employee of that company (such as executives).

All DPSPs must provide for employee vesting. A DPSP does not allow any of the beneficiaries of the plan to be related to a shareholder who owns more than 10% of the voting shares of the company.

The DPSP must set out the effective date of the pension and eligibility of the participants. It must clearly stipulate:

- retirement age;
- death and termination benefits;

- how payments are to be made;
- how the plan can be amended or terminated.

Contributions to a DPSP

Only your employer makes contributions on your behalf. Contributions to a DPSP are made from company profits that the employer shares with you. There may be years when no contributions are made, so DPSPs should not be relied upon as a sole source of your retirement income. However, the contributions and earnings accumulate in the plan on a tax-deferred basis, and can be withdrawn upon retirement or earlier, once the contributions have vested with you.

Contributions are limited to the lesser of 18% of employee earnings for the year or $10,500 for 2008.

The funds in a DPSP are not locked in.

For example, your employer is putting $9,000 a year (the maximum) into your DPSP now. The maximum amount is being indexed at an assumed rate of 2% a year, and you will be retiring in eight years. How much will your DPSP be worth in eight years? Using your financial calculator:

Step	Key	Press	Display will show
1	9,000(+/-)	PMT	-9,000
2	8	N	8
3	2	I	2
4		FV	77,246.72

The DPSP will be worth $77,246.72 in eight years' time when your retirement begins.

Benefits and Withdrawals from a DPSP

The employer must pay all vested amounts to you (or your estate) within 90 days after you terminate your employment or die.

Partial withdrawals from vested funds are possible.

Payments, which must start within 90 days following your retirement or the end of the year of your 71st birthday, whichever is earlier, can be paid to you as:

- a lump sum in cash and/or stock;
- periodic payments for no more than a ten-year period;
- a life annuity.

Taxation of Deferred Profit-sharing Plans

Assets accumulate in a DPSP tax-free, and cannot be transferred, assigned, or used as loan collateral. All benefits are taxed as income. Like RPPs, contributions made by your employer to the DPSP will reduce the amount you can contribute to a Registered Retirement Savings Plan.

A DPSP can be transferred to a Registered Pension Plan (RPP) or an RRSP, or to another DPSP plan, as long as the "new" plan has at least ten members and has existed for one year.

If common shares in a DPSP are transferred to you, any capital gain is not taxed as a benefit to you, but is deferred until you sell the stocks.

Group Retirement Savings Plans (GRSPs)

Group retirement savings plans (GRSPs) provide benefits similar to those offered by individual RRSPs, except your employer, union, or professional association administers them on a group basis. Your contribution by wage deduction is matched wholly or partially by the employer, union, or association. All employer contributions are a taxable benefit to you.

On retirement, a GRSP allows you to choose a life annuity, a registered retirement income fund (RRIF), a cash payment, or a combination of these options.

Like Deferred Profit-sharing Plans, Group Retirement Savings Plans are not "locked in" and can be cashed whenever you decide, depending on the terms of the plan.

Individual Pension Plans (IPPs)

An Individual Pension Plan is a registered pension plan, set up for one person, that specifies the level of payments to the plan holder. It is most suitable for those who are 40 or older and earn an annual salary (T4 income) of more than $100,000 (approximately).

IPPs were designed with business owners in mind. They provide a tax advantage to the member, because contributions are tax-free, and a tax advantage to the business, and because the contributions, set-up, and administrative costs are tax-deductible expenses. When a company borrows funds to make contributions, interest payments are also tax deductible.

The initial contribution to the plan can cover all the unused RRSP contribution room of the IPP member dating back to the incorporation of the firm.

There are two types of IPP:

1. A Shareholder Pension Plan for owner/managers who own more than 10% of the shares of the company.
2. An Executive Pension Plan for new shareholders or those who own less than 10% of the shares of a company. These are often used as an executive perk to attract or retain senior management.

The IPP plan holder may still make a contribution to his or her RRSP or a spouse's plan.

IPP funds are locked-in. As retirement nears, the plan holder can transfer the funds to a locked-in RRSP. This further defers tax until age 71, when the locked-in RRSP must be used to purchase a LIRA, a life annuity, or a Life Income Fund.

Retirement Compensation Arrangements (RCAs)

Like Individual Pension Plans, Retirement Compensation Arrangements are used by:

- owners of privately-held corporations;
- corporate executives making more than $85,000 annually;
- people who might retire outside Canada.

An RCA is established by an employer as a taxable trust. The trust holds the funds for retirement.

Contributions to an RCA are split 50/50 between the trust account and a refundable tax account held by Canada Revenue Agency. The funds that go into the refundable tax account are not invested and are simply returned in the same amounts as they were contributed.

There is no limit to the amount of contribution by the employer. Contributions can be made at any time and invested aggressively, unlike the investment restrictions on registered pension plans. There are many investments eligible for an RCA, including life insurance, stocks and bonds, mutual funds, and deferred annuities. The investments are governed by the trust agreement instead of the *Income Tax Act*.

Funds withdrawn by non-residents are subjected to a 25% withholding tax, unless their country is covered by a tax treaty with Canada. For instance, residents of the United States will pay 15% on withdrawals; a resident of Ireland pays zero in tax.

Supplemental Executive Retirement Plans (SERPs)

A supplemental executive retirement plan is a pension plan that is established for people whose benefits have reached the tax limits of a registered plan. There is no limit on benefits of a SERP. SERPs see highly-paid executives earning the same percentage of their income in their pension as lower-paid workers, because they get around a government cap in pension payouts that affects those earning more than $100,000 per year. That cap means that those earning $500,000 would receive the same pension payout as those earning $100,000.

Unlike regular pension plans that are based on a formula that multiplies a percentage of the employee's base salary by the number of years worked, SERPs include the base salary and bonuses, long-term incentives, and other perks as the basis on which the pension is earned.

Chapter 4

The Process of Retirement Planning: Personal Savings and Investments

Of course, government and company pensions can be supplemented with any savings and investments that you have managed to put together over your working years.

Your options for income from personal savings and investments include:

- your registered plans, such as an RRSP/RRIF;
- a tax-free savings account (TFSA), to come into being in 2009;
- annuities;
- reverse mortgages;
- stocks, Guaranteed Investment Certificates, bonds, and mutual funds;

- insurance products;
- a spousal trust.

Registered Plans

Registered Retirement Savings Plans (RRSPs)

Registered Retirement Savings Plans (RRSPs) were designed to assist individuals in saving for their retirement years. There are two immediate benefits to an RRSP: one is that contributions are tax deductible and the second is that the taxes on the growth of the funds held within the plan are deferred. An RRSP can help you attain a higher standard of living in retirement by supplementing your government or private pension with additional funds.

Investments that earn capital gains and dividends should be held in a non-registered account to take advantage of their special tax treatment (taxed at a lower rate), which will not be enjoyed if they are held in a registered account.

An RRSP is available as a managed or a self-directed plan.

- A **managed plan** is one in which your deposit is invested in products held in trust under the plan. No further investment decisions are required by you.
- In a **self-directed plan**, a bank, trust company, or investment dealer administers your assets. You make all investment decisions.

In both types of plans, you choose from a variety of investments, though self-directed plans have options not available in managed plans.

The funds in the plan can be accessed prior to retirement, and tax must be paid accordingly, both when you withdraw the money and on your income tax return at the end of the year.

Money withdrawn from an RRSP is taxed at your marginal tax rate. This is true regardless of whether it has been generated within the plan as a result of investing in stocks and mutual funds that return capital gains and dividends, or by Guaranteed Investment Certificates that return interest. Thus, you will be motivated to try to reduce your marginal tax rate by using strategies such as income splitting.

Income splitting (described earlier in the book) moves income between spouses, from the spouse with the higher marginal tax rate to the spouse with a lower marginal tax rate. CPP can be split, as can any income you receive to which you are entitled to the $2,000 pension tax credit, such as your RRIF. More information on this subject is provided in the final chapter.

All individuals who have eligible earned income, including non-residents with income earned in Canada may contribute to an RRSP up to December 31 of the year in which they reach age 71. At that point, the RRSP must be cashed-out (and tax paid accordingly) or converted to a Registered Retirement Income Fund or annuity. If the funds are locked-in, because they have come from a registered pension plan, they must be transferred to an equivalent, locked-in plan, which can be accessed after the contributor turns 71.

Designation of a Beneficiary

If you hold an RRSP, you can designate a beneficiary of the plan, who can continue to enjoy the advantage of deferred tax on the funds in the event of your death. These beneficiaries include:

- your spouse;
- dependent children or grandchildren.

On your death, RRSP funds can be transferred tax free to your spouse's own RRSP (if your spouse is younger than 71) or RRIF, or to an annuity in which the spouse is the annuitant.

If any other beneficiary is named, the full value of the plan will be included in your income, even though the funds are paid to the beneficiary.

Calculate the Value of Your RRSP

You can calculate the value of your RRSP in the future by making several assumptions and using the future value of an annuity in the Financial Calculation section.

Example: What will an RRSP with a present value of $30,000, growing at a rate of 7% per year, compounded with an ongoing contribution of $3,000 per year, be worth in 20 years.

Step	Key	Press	Display will show
1	30000(+/-)	PV	-30,000.00
2	7	1	7.00
3	3000(+/-)	PMT	-3,000.00
4	20	N	20.00
5		FV	239,077.01

Answer: $239,077.01

When Your RRSP Matures

You cannot have an RRSP past the end of the year in which you turn 71. You have three options for the money you hold in the plan:

- take it as cash;
- convert it to a Registered Retirement Income Fund (RRIF);
- buy an annuity.

Making this choice has long-lasting ramifications for you and your spouse, and is not a decision that should be made lightly.

Here are some of the factors you will want to consider:

- Do you wish to receive a lower income payment in exchange

for a guaranteed survivor's income that will protect your spouse if you should die first?

- Do you want to generate the highest retirement income from private sources?
- Are you concerned with leaving assets in your estate?

If you are single, without dependents, and are not concerned with leaving an estate, then purchasing a ***straight life annuity*** during a period of high interest rates would be appropriate.

A straight life annuity sees you receive payments until you die. There is no beneficiary.

If you have sufficient retirement income for you and your spouse, even in the event of your death, then term certain annuities or annuities with guaranteed terms or RRIFs are appropriate vehicles for enriching your estate. Those couples who do not have sufficient pension or other guaranteed private retirement income, and who would suffer from the loss of retirement income on the death of either one, should consider acquiring Joint-and-Last-Survivor annuities or transferring their RRSPs into a RRIF.

The choice of the appropriate maturity option will ultimately depend on the amount of retirement income needed to supply you with the necessities of life, whether you or you and/or your spouse will work part time, your intended lifestyle, and any changes in the cost of living associated with your retirement.

Whichever option you choose, you will be taxed on the money you receive at your marginal tax rate.

Most clients will have a mix of registered and non-registered assets. The withdrawal of assets in registered plans should be delayed as long as possible to continue to defer income tax and allow for further compounding. Non-registered assets should be used first.

The marginal tax rate is the rate of tax that applies to the next dollar of income earned. The higher the income level, the higher the marginal tax rate (up to 52% as of 2008).

SPOUSAL CONSIDERATIONS

Spousal contributions to an RRSP can continue after the individual passes the end of the year in which he or she turns 71, if he or she has "earned income," and if the spouse is 71 or younger.

Under Canada Revenue Agency attribution rules, if a spousal RRSP is cashed in and the taxpayer/contributor to the plan has made spousal contributions to it at any time in the past three years, the amount of the cashed-in spousal plan will be taxed in the contributor's hands, not the spouse's. The attribution rule applies to RRIF payments, but only to amounts received in a taxation year that are in "excess of the minimum payment."

Attribution rules dictate who will be taxed for specific types of income splitting. Income splitting is covered in detail in the final chapter of this book.

For example, if John's spouse, Kate, cashes in her RRIF of $10,000, into which John had contributed $6,000 for the past three years ($2,000 in the year the RRIF was purchased and $2,000 for the next two years), $6,000 would be taxed in John's hands and $4,000 in Kate's hands.

RRSP Maturity Options

Option 1: Take It as Cash

This option sees you take out the entire amount of the RRSP as cash. The amount will be fully taxed as income.

This option is appropriate only if the RRSP is very small, or if the plan holder absolutely requires the money to live on.

This is the least favourable of the three maturity options.

Option 2: Purchase an Annuity

When you purchase an annuity, you relinquish control of the funds. As owner of the RRSP you become the annuitant. In return for loss of control, you receive a fixed and regular annuity income from an insurance company. The value of the annuity payment is based upon the interest rate at the time of purchase, and the amount invested in the annuity. The annuity may, or may not, be indexed to inflation.

Annuities are best suited for conservative investors who require an assured monthly income for life.

Remember, an annuity permanently locks the RRSP funds into the interest rates at the time of purchase. Therefore, an annuity is not a good growth investment option, and there may be no protection against inflation. We will provide more information on annuities later in this chapter.

Option 3: Purchase a Registered Retirement Income Fund (RRIF)

This is the most popular maturity option, chosen by over 75% of those converting RRSPs into RRIFs.

The process for conversion is simple: the proper forms are signed and the RRSP funds are transferred into the RRIF account. Other types of deposits cannot be made to a RRIF.

> An annuity can be purchased with RRIF money, but a RRIF cannot be funded from an annuity.

You keep control of your RRIF funds; you also retain some of the same flexibility that existed in the RRSP.

The RRIF pays out regular and gradually increasing payments, until it is exhausted (at about the time you reach age 94).

Registered Retirement Income Funds (RRIFs)

While this section focuses on RRIFs as an RRSP maturity option, it should be noted that you are able to purchase RRIFs at any age. Today's pre-retirees are focused on wealth accumulation leading towards their retirement, and many of them purchase RRIFs as a prudent retirement maturity option, because it gives them the ability to invest in a wider range of investments.

Despite a brief explosion in bond values in the 1980s, over the past 50 years, investments in equities have outperformed all other investments by at least 6.5%—a good reason to continue with equities in your portfolio after retiring.

One of the keys to long-term accumulation of wealth rests with stocks or equity mutual funds. All professional money managers agree that you must have a percentage of your investment asset mix in stocks/equities in order to counter the effects of inflation. In fact, many financial analysts believe the rule of thumb for the best asset mix for wealth accumulation is that the amount in bonds should equal your age, and the balance should be in equities.

Statistics prepared by the Toronto Stock Exchange show that:

- Some 7.5 million Canadians own stock shares, up 23% from nine years ago.
- Share ownership stands second to home ownership.
- The need to grow retirement savings, coupled with prolonged low interest rates, has created a loss of interest in investing in term deposits and savings bonds.
- The "typical"Canadian shareholder is university-educated and receives an average annual income of above $70,000.
- Basically, men look for growth investments; women require security and long-term gains.
- Share owners are focused on retirement planning, tax planning, and Canadian investments.

RRIF Advantages

When your RRSP is rolled over into a RRIF, existing investments continue in their tax-sheltered form, and they maintain the flexibility enjoyed while in the RRSP. A RRIF allows the same investment securities to be held as were in the RRSP, such as mutual funds, stocks, and GICs.

As mentioned, you will receive monthly payments from the RRIF (at a minimally required payment) that continue and increase every year until the RRIF savings are exhausted.

You may hold as many RRIFs as you want. Thus, if GICs are held in multiple institutions within RRIFs, each one will be covered by the Canada Deposit Insurance Corporation to the $100,000 limit.

If you want to withdraw more than the minimum payment, you may do so, and your withdrawal will be subjected to the same withholding tax as RRSP withdrawals.

When you die, you are considered to have received, immediately before death, an amount equal to the fair market value of all property held in the RRIF at the time of death. This amount will be included in the terminal tax return.

If your spouse is named as successor annuitant, the RRIF continues, and your spouse becomes the annuitant. The income your spouse receives is taxed.

RRIFs, Inflation, and Taxation

RRIF investments keep working on a tax-sheltered basis, allowing capital to continue to grow and providing protection against inflation. For instance, if when you retire you need $40,000 worth of income to cover living expenses, and inflation is averaging 2% per year, you will need almost $49,000 per year to pay the same expenses in only ten years' time. In 20 years, a 2% inflation rate means you will need close to $60,000.

A RRIF, however, can be set up to increase cash flow each year to ensure needs are adequately covered. Tax-deferred RRIF investments represent a major wealth-accumulation instrument, because of the power of compounding.

What Inflation Does to $40,000 in Earning Power

Years	2%	3%	4%	5%
0	$40,000	$40,000	$40,000	$40,000
5	$36,157	$32,615	$32,615	$30,951
10	$32,683	$29,497	$26,593	$23,949
20	$26,704	$21,752	$17,680	$14,339

Eligible RRIF Investment Options

The following are RRIF-eligible investments:

- Canada and provincial savings bonds (CSBs);
- federal government Treasury Bills (T-Bills);
- federal, provincial, and municipal government bonds;
- CMHC mortgages and mortgage-backed securities;
- corporate bonds and debentures;
- stripped bonds and coupons;
- Guaranteed Investment Certificates (GICs);
- mutual funds;
- common and preferred shares of Canadian public companies;
- shares of Canadian-controlled private corporations;
- certain rights and warrants;
- call options on certain Canadian public companies;
- shares listed on prescribed foreign exchanges.

Considerations Concerning a RRIF as a Maturity Option

You should start planning for a RRIF before age 71, even though funds will not have to be transferred from your RRSP until it has matured.

It may be appropriate to put the RRIF in your spouse's name, if he or she is younger. In that case, the required legal minimal payout from the plan will be less, since the payments are based upon age. Therefore, though the minimum RRIF payments will be smaller, a larger amount will be left in the RRIF to take advantage of tax-sheltered growth.

This option must be selected when the RRIF is set up.

RRIF CONSIDERATIONS

1. What is your risk-taking personality or profile?
2. How much monthly income must you have to meet your retirement lifestyle expenses?
3. Are there any special expense items for which you should plan?
4. What is a fair estimate of the total of your retirement assets?
5. Do you expect to live for 25 or 30 years after retirement?
6. What are your future expenses (health, emergency, travel)?
7. How much money do you want to leave family members or other causes?
8. Upon retirement, do you want to sell your home and move into an apartment or condominium?
9. What is a reasonable assessment of your total retirement income (RRIFs, public and private pensions)?
10. Should you focus upon investing in interest-bearing investments only, or should you combine them with growth investments in order to offset inflation?

The Four Types of RRIFs Available for Purchase

Savings RRIFs

- the simplest and safest RRIF
- it functions similar to a bank deposit account
- insured by CDIC up to $100,000
- **Disadvantage:** These RRIFs pay the lowest interest rates.

GIC RRIFs

- also a simple form of investment
- insured by CIDC up to $100,000
- pays a better interest rate than savings
- most popular choice of conversion
- **Disadvantage:** Money is locked-in until maturity; it is vulnerable to inflation and changes in interest rates.

Mutual Fund RRIFs

- come in a wide range of options
- professional mutual-fund money managers make all the investment decisions.
- RRIF management/administrative expenses are paid from within the RRIF plan. Paying fees from outside the RRIF could lead to deregistration, and create tax problems, since any money in the RRIF would be regarded as taxable income.
- more growth potential than a savings or GIC RRIF
- provide diversification: RRIF investment is spread over a wide number of securities
- **Disadvantage:** Higher risk element; mutual-fund plans are not covered by deposit insurance; loads and management fees can undermine returns.

Self-Directed RRIFs

- plan holder makes the investment decisions (GICs, bonds, mutual funds, stocks, etc.)
- high growth potential
- plan holder must be comfortable and engaged in managing his or her own investments
- **Disadvantage:** Higher risk than the other types of RRIFs if stocks or equity-based mutual funds are selected.

Withdrawing Funds from the RRIF

RRIFs require minimum annual withdrawals, also called payouts. The minimum annual withdrawal is determined by your age or your spouse's age, the date on which the RRIF was established, and other factors, such as whether the plan has been changed since it was first established. These factors are reflected in the table below, from the Canada Revenue Agency, that shows the minimum withdrawals as a percentage of the value of the plan. Minimum RRIF withdrawals are determined by a schedule in the *Income Tax Act*.

The Canada Revenue Agency classification is based on:

- "Pre-March 1986": this classification is used if the plan was established before March 1986 and has not been changed in any way since that date. Also, there are restrictions for its use if the plan holds an annuity contract.
- "Qualifying RRIFs": used if the plan was established before 1986, but has subsequently been changed, or was established between 1986 and before 1993, or established after 1993 when there has been a transfer from another Qualifying RRIF.
- "All other RRIFs": covers all other possibilities.

The CRA table applies from when the RRIF plan holder or his or her spouse reaches age 71 onward. However, if you or your spouse is 70 or younger, the minimum withdrawal is calculated as: 1 ÷ (90 minus your age or your spouse's) multiplied by the value of the RRIF. For example, if you are 70 with a RRIF valued at \$100,000, the minimum withdrawal will be: 1 ÷ (90 - 70) = .03 x \$100,000 = \$3,333.33.

Minimum RRIF Withdrawal Rates at Various Ages

Age	Pre-March 1986 plan	Qualifying plan	All other RRIFs
71	5.26%	5.26%	7.38%
72	5.56%	5.56%	7.48%
73	5.88%	5.88%	7.59%
74	6.25%	6.25%	7.71%
75	6.67%	6.67%	7.85%
80	10.00%	8.75%	8.75%
84	16.67%	9.93%	9.93%
89	100%	12.71%	12.71%
90	0%	13.62%	13.62%
91	0%	14.73%	14.73%
92	0%	16.12%	16.12%
93	0%	17.92%	17.92%
94+	0%	20.00%	20.00%

Unique Benefit of RRIFs as an RRSP Maturity Option

The use of RRIFs as part of an investment plan provides an extremely important tool for increasing wealth accumulation and savings for retirement because of the diversification of assets they offer.

RRIF investments can be diversified to suit your needs:

- for liquidity → T-Bills
- for security → GICs and bonds
- for growth → mutual funds and securities.

Tip: In order to maximize your wealth accumulation, pay all fees related to plans from funds "outside" the RRIF.

The RRIF investments and the amount allocated to each should be reviewed annually.

Combining RRIFS and Annuities

Under certain circumstances, a combination of RRIFs and annuities may best balance a retirement income plan. Remember, funds may be moved from a RRIF into an annuity at any time.

This combination is attractive because RRIFs provide flexibility and investment growth opportunities, while annuities provide a guaranteed income.

However, those people with extensive registered and non-registered funds and who are attracted to annuities may want to consider purchasing a prescribed annuity with their non-registered funds, while using their registered funds to invest in a RRIF. This can provide a balanced asset mix.

Laddering ("Staggering" Maturities) in a RRIF

Laddering ensures flexibility and a steady income; it also generates the necessary cash flow for withdrawals.

An example of laddering is to buy GICs or bonds so that 20% of the total matures every year, and not at the same time (thus reducing risk and providing some liquidity). Then, reinvest the maturing principal each year for a new five-year term. By doing this, you may benefit from any future increase in interest rates, and you will have the option to reinvest at current interest rates.

Helping You Choose

Financial Situation	Preferred Maturity Option
In addition to several registered assets, you hold sizeable non-registered assets.	RRIF
You require "guaranteed" income to meet your basic living needs.	Annuity
You're able to manage your investment assets to ensure the RRIF lifetime income you require.	RRIF
You worry about inflation and are concerned about outliving your capital.	Annuity
You require absolute control over your assets.	RRIF
Your main objective focuses upon "maximizing" income for life.	Annuity
Your concern is about estate preservation.	RRIF
You don't feel you can manage your assets to ensure the lifetime income you require.	Annuity
Effective tax planning requires you to have income flexibility.	RRIF
Long life expectancy runs in your life, and you are healthy.	Annuity
A primary objective for you is future investment growth.	RRIF
You possess minimal retirement savings	Annuity
You anticipate irregular or increasing income requirements, so you need income flexibility.	RRIF

Your major source of retirement income is RRSPs.	RRIF
Your total retirement income exceeds your expense needs.	RRIF

A Comparison of RRIFs and Annuities

Factors That Point to RRIFs as a Better RRSP Maturity Option Than Annuities

Factor	RRIF	Annuity
Control	You maintain full control.	You lose control of investment options and payments to an insurance company or trust company.
Transfer	You can transfer your RRIF from one institution to another; you can also change your RRIF's content.	You are locked in for the contract's duration.
Flexibility	You decide how much to withdraw each year, subject to the legally required minimum.	No flexibility; you get a fixed regular income sum for a specified period, even if there is inflation.
Inflation	You can minimize inflation by changing your investment strategies (e.g., equity mutual funds, over the long term, perform better than interest-bearing investments), also, you can combine your reinvesting with tax-deferred compounding.	If inflation doesn't remain constant, your invested money erodes; your return/payment is guaranteed, but your investment is locked in.
Rewards	Your invested funds could be higher than your income returns.	Invested funds may return a higher amount than income guarantee.

Locked-in Registered Plans

As we have discussed earlier, those with pension-plan contributions who want to switch their money from the plan, either before or at retirement will have funds that are locked in.

Locked-in funds can generally only be:

- transferred to a LIRA (either managed or self-directed), also known as a Locked-in RRSP;
- transferred to a LIF or LRIF;
- used to buy a deferred life annuity, in which annuity payments would commence at retirement age;
- transferred to a Registered Pension Plan (where the plan permits).

Locked-in Retirement Accounts (LIRAs)

A Locked-in Retirement Account (LIRA) is an account into which pension benefits may be transferred from your employer's plan when you leave the company before retirement. LIRAs are generally subject to the same restrictions on the withdrawal of funds as the original pension plan. On retirement or by the end of the year in which you turn 71, the funds in a LIRA can be used to purchase a life annuity, or transferred to a Life Income Fund (LIF) or a Locked-in Retirement Fund (LRIF).

Life Income Funds (LIFs)

A Life Income Fund (LIF) is a retirement-income fund into which your accumulated savings from a locked-in plan can be transferred at retirement or when your LIRA matures.

LIFs are also referred to as Locked-in RRIFs.

LIFs offer a flexible retirement income option; the principal and income remain tax sheltered until withdrawn, and there is a range of investment options to choose from, similar to those held within an RRSP or LIRA. The owner of the LIF controls the amount of income (within limits) that he or she will receive, and income payments must begin no later than the end of the year after the LIF is opened.

While a RRIF can be opened at any age, a LIF owner must be at least 55 years of age. The earliest date that funds can be transferred to a LIF depends on the province in which the client's pension benefits are deemed to have been earned.

Income-stream options from a LIF are similar to a RRIF in that the plan holder must withdraw a minimum amount each year; a LIF is unlike a RRIF, in that there is a maximum amount that can be withdrawn. The maximum is determined by a formula that applies a term-certain annuity to age 90 to the value of the fund at the beginning of each year. This limit prevents the plan holder from cashing out the plan (unlike a RRIF, which may be cashed out at any time).

Withdrawals from a LIF are subject to a graduated withholding tax when the withdrawal is made, again just like a RRIF. The annuitant must include the total amount withdrawn in his or her income in the year in which the withdrawal is made. The annuitant-taxpayer is credited with the amount of withholding tax already paid.

When a LIF holder dies, the same options are available as with a RRIF plan holder. This includes rolling over the plan to the spouse's RRSP, RRIF, or annuity, tax-free.

Life Retirement Income Fund (LRIF)

The ***Life Retirement Income Fund*** (LRIF) is a variation on the Life Income Fund. LRIFs are currently available in Ontario, Alberta, Manitoba, Newfoundland, and Saskatchewan.

Locked-in funds can be transferred into a LRIF.

The LRIF requires a minimum yearly withdrawal, and there is a cap on the amount that may be withdrawn. The amount of withdrawal is linked to the size of the account.

LIFs AND LRIFs IN ONTARIO

On January 1, 2008, a new LIF was introduced in Ontario to replace the existing LIF and LRIF. The new LIF has more flexible payments and the opportunity for you to withdraw up to 25% of the money transferred into the account if you do so within 60 days of transferring those funds.

The maximum withdrawal made annually from the LIF will see the account exhausted by age 90. However, if you have not taken the maximum amount, the account will continue after you reach age 90, and you can continue to make withdrawals.

The maximum amount you can withdraw is the greater of the amount you would have been paid by the formula (referred to above) or the amount of investment earnings in the account in the previous year.

To acquire a new LIF, you must transfer money from your old LIF. You cannot simply convert one account to the other.

The Tax-free Savings Account (TFSA)

Starting in 2009, people aged 18 and older will be entitled to use a new savings vehicle called the tax-free savings account.

Like RRSPs, the TFSA has a limit to the amount that you can contribute; in 2009 the amount will be $5,000. That figure will be indexed for future years in $500 increments. Unused contribution room can be carried forward, as with an RRSP. The investments in the TFSA can be held in the same investments as an RRSP. On your death, plan assets can be transferred to the TFSA of your spouse or common-law partner.

Unlike RRSPs, the TFSA contribution is not tax deductible, and withdrawals are not taxed.

The TSFA provides a valuable opportunity for tax-free investment growth, while providing retirees with a source of income that will not affect their OAS benefit (because withdrawals are not taxable income). Withdrawals from the TFSA are unlimited.

Comparison of RRSPs/RRIFs and TFSAs

	RRSPs/RRIFs	**TFSAs**
contribution limit (2009)	$21,000	$5,000
tax deductibility of contributions	yes	no
tax on withdrawals	yes	no
tax on investment growth while in the account	no	no

Annuities as a Self-funded Source of Retirement Income

An annuity can form a source of regular income during retirement, and in so doing can provide an equivalent to the income you would receive from a registered pension plan. The primary difference, of course, is that the annuity payments are created by an infusion of *your* capital. The payments you receive will be a combination of capital and interest earned on that capital. Unless you buy a variable annuity, that interest rate is set when you buy the annuity. In times of high interest rates, annuities can appear very attractive.

A variable annuity does not guarantee the same amount of payment over the life of the contract. Therefore it is a variable source of income.

The person who receives the annuity payment or benefit is called the ***annuitant***.

Flow of Capital

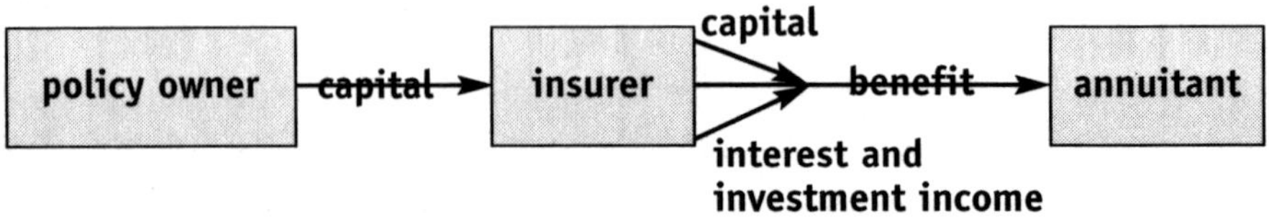

Annuities are available in a registered or a non-registered plan. All income from a registered annuity is taxable; only the interest portion of payments from a non-registered annuity is taxable.

To understand whether an annuity is right for you, you must know the following:

- When do benefits begin?
- Are benefits guaranteed?
- Is there inflation protection?
- Can withdrawals be made, or the contract surrendered?
- What types of annuities are there?
- How many lives are covered?

When Do Benefits Begin?

Annuity benefits can be either immediate, or deferred.

An **immediate annuity** provides its first payment at the end of the first annuity period after you purchase the annuity. If the annuity period is one year, you receive the first benefit one year after the annuity has been purchased. If the annuity period is one month, the first benefit is received one month after the annuity has been purchased. An immediate annuity is typically purchased with a single lump-sum premium, because benefit payments begin so quickly.

An immediate annuity that is non-registered has the advantage of being available in a **prescribed** form.

A prescribed annuity contract spreads your capital evenly over the expected benefit period. The balance of each payment is interest. A non-prescribed annuity contract pays more interest in the early years of the contract and more capital later.

TAXES ON PRESCRIBED AND NON-PRESCRIBED ANNUITIES

For example, monthly annuity benefits are $1,000 for Joseph's annuity. If his annuity is **prescribed**, the payment every month will consist of $875 capital and $125 interest. Tax will be due on the $125. If his annuity is **non-prescribed**, the benefit every month in year two of the contract might consist of $550 capital and $450 interest. Tax will be due on $450. In year ten, the monthly benefit would consist of $895 capital and $105 interest. Tax will be due on $105.

The **total** amount of income tax reported under a prescribed annuity is the same as for a non-prescribed annuity over the duration of the annuity—only the *timing* of the reported income tax differs. If you own a prescribed annuity you will pay the same amount of income tax for your annuity every year over the benefit period, whereas a non-prescribed annuity contract owner will pay more tax in the early years of the contract and then less over time.

The advantages of a prescribed annuity include:

- paying less tax during the contract's early years, since less interest is reported during this period. This leaves you with more net income, which effectively raises the contract's value.
- knowing precisely how much income tax will be reported for tax purposes every year.

To qualify as a prescribed annuity:

- a contract must provide a level benefit, that is, a set amount (except for a joint-and-last-survivor annuity in which payments may be reduced for the surviving annuitant);

- the payments must start within the calendar year following purchase;
- you must own the contract;
- the contract must, if a term-certain annuity, mature no later than age 90. This maturity stipulation applies to the younger of the annuitants when dealing with a joint-and-last-survivor annuity.

If you do not begin receiving benefits until a year or more has passed, then you have a **deferred annuity**. A deferred annuity is not available on a prescribed basis, however it provides unique advantages to you in that the contract can be protected from the claims of creditors.

Deferred annuities offer creditor protection that other forms of managed investment products (such as mutual funds) cannot. Annuities are in many ways like insurance policies. Their creditor protection arises because the ownership in the underlying assets of the annuity resides with the insurance company, and not the policy owner.

A beneficiary of the annuity must be named in order for the annuity to be eligible for creditor protection. In all cases where the beneficiary is revocable, the contract is creditor-protected. However, you may waive this protection where the contract is expressly pledged as security for a loan.

This creditor protection can be an attractive feature for those whose business or personal circumstances expose them to the seizure of assets to satisfy debt.

Deferred annuities and Guaranteed Investment Certificates (GICs) address many of the same investment needs and objectives: security, guaranteed returns, and interest income. The following chart provides a comparison of these investments.

Comparison of a Deferred Annuity with a GIC

	Deferred Annuity	Guaranteed Investment Certificate
Consumer protection	Guaranteed up to $60,000 by Assuris	Guaranteed up to $100,000 by CDIC
Creditor protection	Yes, when a beneficiary has been named	No
Early surrender	Yes, subject to loads and rate adjustments (known as Market Value Adjustment, or MVA)	Often not possible, except under circumstances of great hardship and with hefty penalties
Estate planning	When a beneficiary has been named, proceeds are not subject to probate fees.	Proceeds part of the estate and subject to probate fees, except if held in a registered plan, when it will pass to the named beneficiary.
Partial withdrawals	Yes, subject to loads and rate adjustments (known as Market Value Adjustment, or MVA)	No
Returns	Principal + interest	Principal + interest
Risk	Very low; subject to inflation and interest-rate risk	Very low; subject to inflation and interest-rate risk
RRSP eligibility	Yes	Yes
Taxation	Interest income	Interest income

Are Benefits Guaranteed?

Benefits of an annuity are either fixed or variable.

A **fixed benefit** is guaranteed by the insurer. The benefit is determined by the interest rate offered by the insurer when the annuity contract is written. Each benefit you receive is the same amount of money.

When the benefit is not guaranteed, its amount will vary from payment to payment. This type of payment is called a **variable benefit**; it is received through investment in a variable annuity.

A variable annuity is funded by premiums that buy units in an investment fund. The investment fund invests in common stocks. It is established as an account by the insurer and is separate from other accounts. The value of the fund and its units, therefore, are directly related to stock market performance.

As the stock market moves up and down, the fund and unit values also move up and down. Because the fund and unit values will vary from day to day, so too will the values of a variable annuity and its benefit.

You are not guaranteed to receive a certain amount of *money* from the units, only a certain number of *units*. As the value of these units rises and falls according to the market value of assets held in the investment fund, so too will the benefit derived from the units.

In theory, a variable annuity keeps pace with inflation, because prices of common stocks are expected to keep pace with consumer prices. However, when purchasing a variable annuity, you assume an investment risk that you do not assume when purchasing a fixed-benefit annuity contract.

Inflation Protection

An **indexed annuity** provides for payments to increase; its purpose is to provide a hedge against inflation. The payment rates are influenced and increased according to increases in the index to which they are tied (e.g., the cost of living index). However, if the annuity is purchased with registered funds (e.g., a RRSP), by law indexing cannot exceed 4% per year.

Can Withdrawals Be Made from an Annuity?

Immediate annuities are available in **commutable** form—in which you can cancel the annuity before the contract maturity date and convert the balance of unpaid payments to a lump-sum payment—or in **non-commutable** form, in which they cannot be paid out.

The commutable annuity contract will set out when you can utilize this option. Some contracts allow you to make the withdrawal at any time, or if you can establish a case of extreme hardship. The actual amount you can withdraw will be based upon the present value of the unpaid benefits, discounted to allow for the time value of money.

Deferred annuities allow early withdrawals, and many insurers include a back-end load in these contracts, so you actually pay a fee if you make a withdrawal. This fee serves two purposes: it covers initial expenses and is a disincentive for early withdrawals. The load is quite often based on a percentage of funds withdrawn, and may decline over the term of the annuity, until the withdrawal charge no longer applies.

Because there is a period between the date the annuity is purchased and the beginning of deferred annuity payments, there is a period of time during which the value of the deposit grows. This is called the ***accumulation period***, and the increase in value is called the ***accumulated value***. The accumulated value is the net amount paid for the annuity, plus interest. The amount of interest earned depends on whether the annuity is a fixed or variable-benefit annuity.

Deferred annuity contracts usually give you the right to withdraw all or a portion of the annuity's accumulated value during the accumulation period.

The amount you can withdraw from a fixed-benefit contract is known in advance, but when you are dealing with a variable annuity, the amount that you can withdraw at any given time during the accumulation period is determined by the market value of the assets in the investment fund that underlies the variable contract. This valuation is done daily. Thus, you cannot know the amount with complete certainty.

Insurers may allow one withdrawal without a charge, so long as that withdrawal does not exceed a set percentage of the fair market value of the assets held in the annuity. For example, a person with an annuity with a fair market value of $50,000 may have a contract that allows a free withdrawal of up to 10% of the fair market value of the contract without payment of a penalty or withdrawal charge. Thus, the person could make a one-time withdrawal of up to $5,000.

When an annuity contract is surrendered, or an early withdrawal is made, an adjustment will be made to the interest rate on which the fixed-benefit annuity is based. This is termed a ***market value adjustment (MVA).***

A market value adjustment is basically a penalty that reflects any changes in the interest rate between the time the contract was taken out and the time it is being surrendered. This information should be sought from the company that holds the annuity for you.

What Types of Annuities Are Available?

Annuities provide an income for a specified period of time, called a term, or for life.

Term-Certain Annuities

Whereas most people are familiar with term life insurance that provides life insurance coverage for a specified period of time or to a specified age, they may be less knowledgeable about ***term-certain annuities***. Term-certain annuities provide an income for a specified time or to a specified age.

A term-certain annuity, also known as an ***annuity certain*** or a ***fixed-term annuity***, pays you a guaranteed income for either:

- a defined period of time (e.g., 5 years);
- a period ending at a specified age, e.g., age 85, at which time the annuity matures; or
- a specified period, equal to the number of years from your age at purchase to age 90, or until your spouse turns 90.

A term-certain annuity can be bought with either a single premium (a lump sum) or a series of premiums over a period of time. If you die before the term is completed, the income is paid to your beneficiary, either for the balance of the term, as a lump sum, or to your estate.

A TERM-CERTAIN ANNUITY

Jane Morgan buys a term-certain annuity for $50,000 when she is 55, naming herself as annuitant. She wants to begin receiving the annuity payments when she is 65, and she specifies the maturity date of the annuity to be when she is 75. Jane's annuity is therefore a 10-year deferred-term-certain annuity. Jane has specified she wants to receive a monthly income during the ten years she receives the annuity. Jane will be paid a defined benefit: each month she will receive a portion of the $50,000 she used to buy the annuity, plus interest, at a rate that the insurer has guaranteed.

A term-certain annuity provides complete security. You know in advance both how *long* you will be receiving income, how *much* you will receive, and *when*. Annuity payments can be received monthly, quarterly, bi-annually, or annually.

A Life Annuity

A ***life annuity*** makes income payments for your entire lifetime. In this way, it is similar to permanent insurance that provides life insurance for the entire lifetime of the insured. Like permanent insurance, a life annuity is *only* available from an insurer.

Once payments from a life annuity begin, they cannot be stopped or converted into a lump-sum payment. They will continue as income until you die.

Although all life annuity payments are based on an annuity rate (amount per $1,000 of the purchase price), these rates vary according to:

- the form and frequency of payment (monthly, quarterly, semi-annually, or annually);
- your age and gender (because women live longer than men, their life annuity payments would extend for a longer period);
- the interest rate at the time of purchase;
- your medical history as annuitant, including whether you are a smoker.

There is often a significant difference in annuity rates offered by different insurers, despite the fact that they must all deal with the same variables—investment rates of return, actuarial assumptions, and actuarial expenses. Accordingly, you should look for the best annuity rate by doing some comparative shopping.

The most common types of life annuities are:

- life-straight annuities (also called life only);
- life annuities with a guaranteed number of payments (also called life annuity with period certain);

- joint-and-last-survivor annuities;
- installment-refund annuities;
- cash-refund annuities.

Life-Straight Annuity

Life-straight annuities pay a *guaranteed* income for life. They end with your death, regardless of how long you live. These annuities pay the highest benefit per $1,000 of purchase price. This is because no extra reserve needs to be set aside by the insurance company for beneficiaries. They are attractive to those who want the highest income possible or those who do not have dependents who would be beneficiaries.

EXAMPLE

Joseph Hassoun buys a life-straight annuity that guarantees him a monthly income of $1,250 for the rest of his life. Whether Joseph dies in one year or 30 years, his daughter, Resa, his sole beneficiary, will not receive any payment from the annuity.

Life Annuity with a Guaranteed Number of Payments

Similar to a life-straight annuity, this type of annuity provides an income that is guaranteed for a specified period of time (e.g., 5, 10, or 20 years), or until your death after that period of time. If you die before the end of this period, the balance of the benefits will be paid to your beneficiary until the guarantee period ends. If you live longer than the specified period of time, the benefit continues until the last installment you are paid before your death, and then nothing more is paid. These annuities pay less than life-straight annuities, since the insurer runs the risk that you will live longer than the specified period of time.

EXAMPLE

Joseph Hassoun buys a life annuity with a guaranteed number of payments that will pay $1,000 a month for life for a 10-year guaranteed period. (Note: the amount he receives is less than a straight-life annuity, because of the guarantees provided.) If he dies in year seven of the annuity, his beneficiary will receive $1,000 a month for the next three years, when the annuity matures. If Joseph lives for another six years, he will continue to receive his monthly benefit until he dies, but no payment will be made to his beneficiary.

Installment Refund Annuity

An installment-refund annuity guarantees a set number of income payments equal to the purchase price. If you die before receiving the purchase price of the annuity, your beneficiary will receive an amount equal to the difference between the guarantee and what was received, paid in installments.

EXAMPLE

Norm Hooper buys an installment-refund annuity with $100,000 that he has received as an inheritance. Norm dies after receiving only $55,000 in annuity payments. His beneficiary receives $45,000 in **installment** payments.

Cash-Refund Annuity

A cash-refund annuity guarantees you an income for life. If you die before receiving payments equal to the purchase price of the annuity, the difference between the purchase price and the total amount received is paid to either a beneficiary or to your estate in a lump sum.

Comparing Life Annuities

	Income Paid	No. of annuitants	After death of annuitant
Life Straight Annuity	For life of annuitant	One	No payment to beneficiary
Life Annuity with a Guaranteed Number of Payments	For a specified period or until death of annuitant after that period	One	If death occurs during specified period, payments continue to beneficiary for balance of period; if death occurs after specified period, no payments to beneficiary
Joint-and-Last-Survivor Annuity	For lifetimes of two annuitants	Two	On death of one annuitant, the other receives entire income; on death of surviving annuitant, no payment to beneficiary
Installment-Refund Annuity	The amount of income will equal the purchase price	One	If income received is less than purchase price of annuity, the difference between income and purchase price is paid to beneficiary in installments
Cash-Refund Annuity	For life of annuitant	One	If income received is less than purchase price of annuity, the difference between income and purchase price is paid to beneficiary in a lump sum

EXAMPLE

Norm Hooper buys a cash refund annuity with $100,000 that he has received as an inheritance. Norm dies after receiving only $55,000 in annuity payments. His beneficiary receives $45,000, in a **lump-sum** payment.

Coverage of More than One Life

A joint-and-last-survivor annuity is a life annuity that provides a guaranteed income during the course of two people's lives. On your death, the entire income is paid to the survivor for the remainder of his or her life. Typically used by spouses, this annuity can be purchased by any two persons.

EXAMPLE

Jill and John buy a joint-and-last-survivor annuity. They receive $1,000 per month. At the death of Jill or John, the survivor will continue to receive $1,000 per month. When the survivor dies, there is no payment to a beneficiary.

Calculate the Amount of Income from an Annuity

You can roughly calculate the income you might expect from an annuity by using the steps we showed you in the section of Calculations.

Example:
What is the annual income of a term-certain annuity worth $239,077.01, assuming a 5% annual rate of return and a 15-year term?

Step	Key	Press	Display will show
1	239077.01	PV	-239,077.01
2	5	I	5.00
3	15	N	15.00
4		PMT	23,033.23

Answer: $23,033.23

Reverse Mortgages as a Source of Income

A reverse mortgage is a type of loan that is used to convert the equity in a home into cash. Retirees who find themselves cash poor and house rich can use the money obtained through a reverse mortgage to achieve financial security at the expense of their estate value.

The amount advanced under the mortgage (up to 50% of the home value) depends on the value of your home, your age, and your marital status. The proceeds may be taken as a lump sum, as guaranteed monthly payments, or as a combination of the two.

Essentially, a reverse mortgage is the reverse of a conventional mortgage. Instead of you paying the lender each month, the lender pays you.

The principal amount of the loan, along with accumulated interest, is due when you pass away or sell the home. There is no requirement for monthly repayments, but there is the option of paying off the loan and accumulated interest at an earlier date, along with penalties.

The payments received are taxable, however, the interest that accumulates on the loan is tax deductible, and usually offsets any tax payable.

Using funds from a reverse mortgage, rather than those from an RRSP, allows you to take continued advantage of those government plans (e.g., GIS, OAS) that are based on levels of income.

Reverse mortgages have legal, appraisal, and closing costs to consider. If interest rates are not fixed, they float and tend to be on the high side. When property values fall, the amount owing on a straight reverse mortgage could exceed the value the property would bring when sold.

Personal Savings and Investments

Income from Investments

Investment income in non-registered accounts is an important source of funds for retirees. Issues for retirees in regard to investment income typically centre on the ease with which the investments themselves can be redeemed and whether the investments are guaranteed.

Detailed information on investing and investments is available in the companion book *What Your Financial Advisor Knows—and You Should Know Too). . . About Investing for Retirement and Taxes.*

Guaranteed Investment Certificates (GICs)

Guaranteed Investment Certificates are a popular investment choice, because they are easy to buy, their principal and interest are guaranteed, and they offer a variety of terms and rates. Further, you can use them as collateral for a loan, and they are automatically renewed at maturity.

GICs are available in both redeemable and non-redeemable forms; the non-redeemable GIC cannot be cashed before maturity, except in the case of death or extreme hardship.

Two disadvantages associated with GICs is that they are not all RRSP eligible and they are not covered by the Canada Deposit Insurance Corporation if their term is longer than five years.

Canada Deposit Insurance Corporation covers bank accounts and GICs of less than five years' duration with $100,000 in insurance if the financial institution becomes insolvent.

The interest earned in a GIC is taxable as income.

The returns from a GIC can be improved by employing a strategy called laddering. Laddering sees the principal invested in equal portions, with each portion earning a rate of interest and maturing at different times. As a portion matures, it may be reinvested or redeemed.

GICs are available as:

- **Escalating-Rate GIC:** the interest rate increases over the term.
- **Installment GIC**: an initial contribution is followed by additional contributions.
- **Interest-Rate-Linked GIC**: the interest rate is linked to changes in the prime rate or other interest or money-market rates.
- **Index-Linked GIC**: combines the safety of a guaranteed deposit with the growth potential of an equity instrument. These are popular with conservative investors who want safety but also higher yield potential from standard term deposits. These GICs are insured through the Canada Deposit and Insurance Commission (CDIC) in the same way as regular fixed-rate GICs.
    - They are linked to either a domestic stock-market index or a global stock-market index.
    - Terms vary: some are linked to the index on a specific date and others are linked to the index over a period of time. Other options include locking in the return achieved as of a certain date or allowing early redemptions (e.g., anniversary dates).

- Returns on these GICs are considered income for tax purposes, and it is not unusual for the return to be capped below the potential return of the index. Investors do not receive dividends.
- In a market downturn, investors will receive the guaranteed fixed-interest portion, which is usually less than that of a regular GIC. Thus, there is a limit to the downside risk, but also a limit to the upside potential.

Income Trusts

Income trusts are similar to a closed-end mutual fund in that you purchase an ownership interest in the trust and all revenue and expenses of the trust flow through to you. In the past, trusts distributed their earnings to investors, who, in turn, paid taxes on the income. New regulations introduced in 2006 leave trusts with less to give out to investors. Most income trusts do not trade over the counter or on an exchange.

Since trust expenses are usually higher than income earned in the early years of the trust, these trusts are often used as a tax-deferral strategy for higher-income investors.

The trusts hold properties (e.g., real estate) or assets (e.g., oil and gas projects) to produce income.

They are somewhat similar to bonds, because of the income they produce, but there are no guaranteed payouts.

Real-Estate Investment Trusts (REITs)

The assets of real-estate investment trusts are pooled and are used to invest in and manage a portfolio of commercial properties.

Investors buy units in the trust. REITs enable small investors to make investments in commercial real estate that would not normally be available to them.

REITs may be either open- or closed-ended, and qualify for RRSPs, RRIFs, and DPSPs (Deferred Profit-Sharing Plans).

Advantages of REITs

REITs are highly liquid, significantly more liquid than an investment in real estate.

REITs are typically traded on stock exchanges. They trade like a fixed-income security: when interest rates rise, the market price falls. This means that they provide a hedge against inflation, since in an inflationary market, the underlying real-estate value may rise.

Possible disadvantages: of REITs

REITs trade on yields, and generally have high income yields, but they lack significant capital-gains potential.

Since Canadian REITs are trusts, investors can have environmental liability from the REIT's ownership of certain types of commercial real estate (e.g., if the REIT owned gas bars). For this reason, they carry insurance.

Natural disasters such as floods or tornadoes can pose a risk both to properties and to the levels of insurance costs.

Stocks

Income from stocks will be generated both by trading and from dividends. Neither form of income is guaranteed.

Trades in common and preferred shares settle three business days following the day of the trade (T + 3). Trading stocks will produce capital gains and capital losses for the share owner. Capital gains are taxed at the lowest level of all types of income.

Both forms of income from stock ownership receive preferential tax treatment. Capital gains that come from selling stock for more than you paid is taxed at the lowest rate. Dividends are taxed at a rate higher than capital gains but lower than interest income.

A corporation may pay a portion of company profits to shareholders as a dividend; they are, of course, also not guaranteed, and so cannot be relied upon as a source of income. Dividends also receive preferential tax treatment compared to interest income.

Preferred stock or preferred shareholders are entitled to special privileges not available to holders of common stock. Generally, preferred shareholders receive a regular dividend of an amount specified when the shares are issued (as long as there are sufficient profits to distribute the dividend).

Preferred dividends are usually cumulative, that is, unpaid preferred dividends accumulate and must be paid before any dividends are paid to the common shareholders.

- *Participating preferred* shares pay the preferred dividend plus the common share dividend.
- *Convertible preferred* shares may be converted to another type of share (usually common shares) of the corporation under certain conditions.
- *Redeemable preferred* shares may be redeemed at the corporation's option at a set price and under certain conditions.

Bonds

The maturity dates for bonds are specified as money-market (due in less than one year), short term (five years to maturity), medium term (five to ten years to maturity), and long term (more than ten years to maturity).

Bonds either have coupons attached, which can be detached and cashed, or will pay interest by cheque. When the coupons have been removed from the bond, it is called a stripped bond. Bonds, for the most part, are considered guaranteed investments, since the investor knows the amount of interest the bond will yield. Only bonds of lower quality do not provide the same assurance.

A ***callable*** or ***redeemable*** bond has a call, or redemption, feature that gives the issuer the right to pay off the bond before the maturity date.

Canada Savings Bonds (CSBs)

CSBs are a highly liquid investment, because, after an initial three months, during which no interest is earned, they can be cashed at any bank at any time at their full value plus accrued interest.

No interest is earned for the calendar month in which the bonds are redeemed. They are guaranteed.

Treasury Bills (T-Bills)

T-bills are short-term obligations in $1,000, $5,000, $25,000, $100,000, or $1-million denominations. Their terms to maturity are 91 days, 182 days, and 364 days.

Instead of paying interest, T-bills:

- are sold at a discount;
- mature at par (i.e., $100);
- provide a guaranteed return that is the difference between the issue price and par price.

Mutual Funds

Mutual funds provide all three types of non-guaranteed investment income—interest, dividends, and capital gains. Mutual funds are widely available through insurance-company subsidiaries, banks, and investment dealers. When a unitholder wants to redeem shares, this can be accomplished quickly and easily.

The right of withdrawal or the right of redemption gives mutual-fund unitholders the ongoing right to withdraw their investment from a fund at any time. The fund pledges to buy back these units at the actual liquidating value or redemption value. The amount that the purchaser may recover is the net asset value of the units at the time of the redemption, minus any sales charges.

If the purchase price does not exceed a specified amount ($50,000 in Ontario), the purchaser of a mutual fund has the right to rescind or cancel a lump-sum purchase. However, notice must be given to the organization from which the purchase was made within two business days after the purchaser receives the prospectus or the written confirmation of the purchase.

Typically the return on a mutual fund is not guaranteed, although a relatively new type of mutual fund called a life-cycle mutual fund does, in some cases, provide a guaranteed return. Life-cycle funds are designed with a target end date, the date on which the fund will end or mature. As this date approaches, the overall asset allocation of the fund automatically adjusts to become more conservative. This helps investors take advantage of market growth opportunities early on in their investments, while protecting the value of the fund as it gets closer to maturity.

Insurance Products as a Source of Income

The Leveraged Deferred Compensation Plan

The Leveraged Deferred Compensation Plan (LDCP) combines the benefits of a universal life insurance policy with a loan to provide an income in retirement. The LDCP is a way to grow a **tax-sheltered** investment; it allows clients to tap into the value of a life insurance policy tax free while they are still alive. It does not allow the payment of tax-free benefits until after death.

How the LDCP Works

Firstly, if you are seeking to use the LDCP, you take out a universal-life insurance policy. Universal life insurance is comprised of term life insurance with a savings or investment fund that is sheltered from tax. Then, on retirement, you use the investment value of the policy as collateral for a loan from a financial institution. The financial institution advances payments to you free of tax. Interest on the loan is charged at the going rate (e.g., prime + 1/2% to 1%), and it can be accumulated or paid yearly. As interest accumulates, the amount of the loan increases while the value of the life insurance to the estate decreases.

Finally, on your death, the policy proceeds are used to pay the loan plus interest; the remaining value of the policy is paid out tax free to the policy beneficiaries.

The LDCP works best for a client who:

- is in a high tax bracket;
- is not risk-averse;
- needs life insurance;
- has used all RRSP contribution room;
- has other investments to supplement retirement income;
- is sophisticated and understands the full implications of the arrangement.

The risks of the LDCP are:

- a change to tax laws. Currently, the universal-life policy can be used as collateral without a deemed disposition (e.g., the policy is not treated as though it has been "sold"). The Canada Revenue Agency might change the rules and require the property to be treated for tax purposes as if there had been a deemed disposition on the date of the first payment. A deemed disposition would incur significant tax liability for the policy owner.

- the reluctance of the financial institution to accept the insurance policy as collateral. Making the loan arrangements when the policy is arranged will avoid this problem.
- the LDCP needs at least ten years to work. In the early years, premiums will go mostly towards the cost of insurance, leaving little for actual investment growth. If you are too close to retirement when you buy the insurance policy, there may be insufficient growth.
- loan interest rates and the rates of return on investments may change to make the LDCP less attractive. The difference between the two rates can have a great effect on the outcome. When a wealth manager assumes a **large** difference between the two rates, the LDCP appears **less** risky. Conversely, when a **small** difference is assumed, the LDCP appears to have **greater** risk.
- this strategy is attractive if you have many years before retirement but the length of time between proposing the LDCP and actual retirement means an even greater chance of inaccuracy in projections (e.g., on what the rate of interest on the loan will be and what the rate of return on the investment will be).

The LDCP is a leveraged investment; as such, it carries additional risk. You should consult with your advisor before proceeding with such a plan.

Insured Annuity

An insured annuity is essentially a prescribed life annuity and a term-to-100 life insurance policy, purchased together. The combination of the benefits provided by these products is ideal for you if you are seeking guaranteed income and the preservation of your capital.

Term-to-100 life insurance is a permanent policy that will be in force until you die. It is the least expensive form of permanent insurance.

How an Insured Annuity Works

Using your capital, you buy a life annuity, and at the same time take out a term-to-100 life insurance policy with a death benefit equal to the value of the life annuity. So, if you used $500,000 to buy the life annuity, the insurance policy will have a $500,000 death benefit. You receive a guaranteed income stream from the annuity and use a portion of your regular annuity payments to pay the premiums on the life insurance policy. Upon your death, the annuity ends and the death benefit of the life insurance policy is paid directly to your named beneficiary, tax free.

Even if you have health-related issues that drive up the cost of the premiums on the life insurance, the very same health reasons will mean that your annuity payment will be higher, because your life expectancy is lower.

An insured annuity pays a higher guaranteed after-tax income for life compared to most traditional alternatives, while preserving your capital for your heirs.

Cash Surrender Values and Withdrawals from Life Insurance Policies

Life insurance comes in two basic forms: term insurance and permanent insurance. We have already discussed one type of permanent policy, term-to-100, in regards to its use in insured annuities. There are two other forms of permanent insurance that have relevance to retirees seeking sources of funds. They are whole-life insurance and universal-life insurance.

Both of these policies develop a cash value from the premiums that are paid to keep the policies in force; the cash value can be accessed as a lump sum or it can be annuitized. Annuitization converts the cash value into an annuity.

When you take the cash value, you surrender the policy, which is where the name *cash surrender value* came from. Whether you take the money or convert the policy to an annuity, there will be a taxable gain that you must declare as income in the year you receive the funds.

You calculate the taxable gain by taking the adjusted cost basis for the policy—basically how much was paid in premiums—and subtracting from that amount the cost of your life insurance coverage. You then subtract this sum from the cash surrender value and the taxable gain is the amount that remains.

As the owner of a universal life insurance policy, you are permitted to make a cash withdrawal from your policy and still keep the policy in force. Your death benefit will however be reduced by the amount of the withdrawal.

Again, a taxable event is created; the formula to calculate the amount of tax that will be owed is quite complicated, and it is best to check with a tax expert or life insurance agent on this before proceeding.

A Spousal Trust

We looked at this earlier in the book. You would receive income from a spousal trust if your spouse created the trust during his or her lifetime, though it would not be until he or she died that assets would flow into the trust for your benefit.

If you are the **sole** beneficiary, assets transfer to the trust tax free. The assets are considered the capital of the trust; the income created by those assets will form the income you receive from the trust. You must receive all of the income of the trust during your lifetime; no other person may obtain or use the income or capital of the trust while you live. The trust will be administered by a trustee, and it will be the job of the trustee to ensure assets are not depleted, as they might be by a spouse who spends irresponsibly or capriciously. On your death, the capital can be inherited by beneficiaries of the trust.

Spousal trusts are used to take advantage of tax savings and to protect the estate assets in the event that the surviving spouse remarries.

A SPOUSAL TRUST

Mark is concerned that his wife, June, might remarry after his death and her new husband might spend everything June had inherited from Mark, leaving nothing for their two children. Mark has the option of distributing his estate, one-third to June and one-third to each of his two children, or setting up a spousal trust in his will. With the spousal trust, during her lifetime June will be the income beneficiary of the assets that have been transferred into the trust tax free, and the children will become the capital beneficiaries when June dies.

June would live off the income for her lifetime and, when she dies, the trust will pass to the children without probate.

Chapter 5

How Much Do You Need?

Of course, the big "nut" to crack is that, now that you know where the money can come from, how much of it will be required?

How Much Money Is Needed?

There are five steps in the process of finding out how much money you are going to need and how much you need to save to arrive at that figure:

1. Assess the variables that will have an impact your retirement.
2. Estimate the dollar amount that will be necessary to fund a standard of living in retirement that is a comparable to that which you currently enjoy.

3. Calculate your sources of income and their impact on your needs.
4. Determine the value of what you have accumulated so far.
5. Convert the sum needed into an annual savings objective.

Assess the Variables

This is where you are going to gaze into your crystal ball and make some really good guesses about:

- how many years there will be until you retire;
- your life expectancy and that of your spouse;
- the expected rate of inflation;
- the return on your investments.

Clearly none of these can be known in advance, but you need to pull these numbers together to allow you to make the financial estimates that follow this step.

Years Until Retirement

This period is called the accumulation period. It is important for two reasons: one, the more time you have available, the more you can save and, two, as you approach retirement, the more conservative your investment strategy typically becomes. This is not just because as you age you become less likely to take risk, but because you simply may not have time to make up losses.

Life Expectancy

People are living longer. As of 2005, Statistics Canada reported that the average life expectancy for Canadian men was 78 and for women 82.7. What this means is that if your retirement takes place at age 65, you must still plan for a minimum of 13 or 17.7 years in retirement. A conservative projection would assume 20 and 25 years.

Rate of Inflation

Inflation is the insidious upward creeping of costs. In June 2008, the Bank of Canada recorded the rate of inflation at 3.1%. If the rate was just 3%, your annual living expenses of $50,000 today will cost $87,700 in twenty years. Thus, retirement income planning must take into account an ever-increasing need for income.

Retirement income planning must also consider the erosion in value that will occur to fixed-income assets over time (e.g., a pension plan or annuity that does not provide cost-of-living increases). If your pension in 2008 accounts for half of your living expenses today($25,000), in twenty years, it will provide only about 28% of your living expenses. This means you will face a 22% shortfall that you must make up through other means.

Inflation is a variable that is difficult to predict but should not be underestimated.

The Return on Your Investments

Fortunately, working in opposition to inflation is the growth of your invested funds through interest or an increase in their value. So, as inflation is demanding you spend more money, the return on your investments will hopefully keep pace with or surpass the rate of inflation. The power of compounding to achieve this objective cannot be overstated.

Albert Einstein considered compounding to be the eighth wonder of the world.

Tax deferral is another powerful tool to enhance your investment return, and one of the great benefits of an RRSP. When you leave money in the account, tax deferred, it will provide a large base from which compounding occurs.

Investment return is also a difficult variable to predict. The best approach is to be conservative in your estimates and revisit your projections regularly to update returns as needed.

Estimate Your Retirement Income Need

There are two ways to estimate how much income you will need during retirement:

- as a percentage of pre-retirement income;
- on the basis of projected expenses.

The percentage-of-income method is a quick "rule of thumb" approach that stipulates you will need 70% to 90% of pre-retirement income to produce a standard of living that is comparable to the one you enjoy today.

Determining your need based on projected expenses is far more accurate. It requires you compile your annual costs for:

- housing;
- utilities;
- taxes, both property and income;
- transportation;
- personal expenses, such as food, clothing, hobbies, sports;
- charitable donations;
- medical expenses;
- insurance, both property, life, and health,
- entertainment;
- travel;
- savings;
- dependents, including children and aging parents.

The closer you are to retirement, the more accurate your projection will be. You may even want to take this a step further by categorizing your income needs according to the near term (the first eight or ten years of retirement), the mid term (the following seven or eight years), and the far term (thereafter). Costs that may be low in the near term, such as the medical insurance needed by those who travel out of the country, may take on far more financial significance in the mid- to long term. The reverse will also be true. As time goes on, your expenses for travel and dependents are likely to diminish.

> Remember you are making this estimate using today's dollars. You need to calculate an inflation factor to make the estimate more accurate for the future.

Now this is where your financial calculator is going to prove invaluable. Using the chart below simply fill in:

- the amount of today's living expenses;
- the period of time that you are planning towards;
- a rate of inflation.

Step	Key	Press	Display will show
1		PV	
2		N	
3		I	
4		FV	

If you haven't mastered the calculator, here are some dollar amounts for you to ponder, based on an inflation rate of 3%.

Future Living Expenses

Your estimated living expenses for retirement	In 5 years, these living expenses will be	In 10 years, these living expenses will be	In 20 years, these living expenses will be
$30,000	$34,778	$40,317	$54,183
$40,000	$46,371	$53,757	$72,244
$50,000	$57,964	$67,196	$90,306
$60,000	$69,556	$80,635	$108,367
$70,000	$81,149	$94,074	$126,428
$80,000	$92,742	$107,513	$144,489
$90,000	$104,335	$120,952	$162,550
$100,000	$115,927	$134,392	$180,611

Your Sources of Income

Now that we've looked at the outgoing scenario, let's see how your sources of income relate to it.

This is simple enough to estimate:

- Take your estimated living expenses for retirement.
- Subtract all government sources of income.
- Subtract your pension amount, as shown on your pension statement.

The number you are left with is your annual income need.

This bottom-line number is the retirement income that you must generate through your RRSPs and non-registered savings. Again, you can use your financial calculator to arrive at this number.

Example:

Luciano estimates he and his wife will require $30,000 gross income in retirement, and will receive $12,000 in government benefits. They have no other sources of income in retirement. Assuming a 4% withdrawal rate, how much will they require in savings when they retire?

Step	Key	Press	Display will show
1	30000	-	30,000.00
2	12000	=	18,000.00
3		÷	
4	4%	=	450,000.00

Answer: $450,000.00

The following table will provide an overview based on 20 years of retirement, and investment returns of 5%, 7%, and 9%. These figures assume that your annual income need increases at 3% per year. It shows, for instance, that you will need $1,000,000 to fund retirement of 20 years' duration if you achieve a 7% return on your investments.

Money Needed to Fund 20 Years' Retirement

Income need per year	@ 5% return on investments	@ 7% return on investments	@ 9% return on investments
$25,000	$400,000	$333,000	$282,000
$50,000	$800,000	$667,000	$565,000
$75,000	$1,200,000	$1,000,000	$850,000
$100,000	$1,597,000	$1,333,000	$1,130,000

The Value of What You've Accumulated

Now, let's see what your current savings will amount to; with any luck they will reduce the amount of money that you will need very substantially.

Again, your financial calculator will provide you with an accurate and personalized projection.

Example:

Phelim is 50 years old, and has $100,000 in personal savings. He hopes to retire in 15 years, and would like to know what his savings will be worth at that time. He estimates optimistically that his savings will earn 9% over the next 15 years. What will Phelim's savings be worth at retirement?

Step	Key	Press	Display will show
1	100000(+/-)	PV	100,000.00
2	15	N	15.00
3	9	I	9.00
4		FV	364,248.25

Example: $364,248.25

Again, here's an overview for you, in case you have not mastered the calculator:

The Future Values of $10,000

$10,000	@ 3%	@ 5%	@ 7%
In 3 years	10,922	11,576	12,250
In 5 years	11,593	12,763	14,026
In 7 years	12,299	14,071	16,058
In 10 years	13,439	16,289	19,672
In 12 years	14,258	17,959	22,522
In 15 years	15,580	20,789	27,590
In 20 years	18,061	26,533	38,697

Converting the Sum into Annual Savings

Finally, you will estimate the annual savings needed to meet this objective.

Example:

Phelim decides that he wants savings worth $700,000 at retirement. What does he need to save per year to reach this objective, given the same assumptions above?

Step	Key	Press	Display will show
1	335751.75	FV	335,751.75
2	15	N	15.00
3	9	I	9.00
4		PMT	-11,435.33

Answer: $11,435.33

And, here's an overview of how much you must save each year to fund a retirement income need of $50,000:

When $50,000 Is the Objective			
Savings available	$1,000,000	$714,285.71	$555,555.56
Accumulation Period	@ 4%	@ 7%	@ 9%
10 years	$79,504.58	$51,698.22	$36,566.72
20 years	$30,242.59	$17,423.52	$10,859.15
30 years	$15,051.44	$7,561.72	$4,075.75
40 years	$8,278.16	$3,577.96	$1,644.23

Investing for Retirement

As retirement approaches, your time horizon for investing decreases. This inevitably causes people to become more cautious with their investments; they can't afford to lose returns, however small. This is the point at which asset allocation—that is, how much you have divided among the various asset classes of cash, fixed-income securities, and equities amongst others—must be adjusted to reflect your lower tolerance for losses.

A good strategy to put in place is to lock an ever-greater amount of the investment portfolio into cash and fixed-income investments as retirement approaches. In this way the principal is protected, as well as returns that have been achieved to date.

The best investments for this purpose are T-bills, money-market mutual funds, short-term Guaranteed Investment Certificates, and Canada Savings Bonds. Segregated funds can also work to this end, providing you have a ten-year window before you need the money that is invested in the funds.

It is advisable to work with your financial advisor to find the best products for your needs.

Chapter 6

Taxation Issues Related to Retirement Planning

We've remarked on many issues relating to taxes throughout the preceding pages, including the tax status of the various forms of income you may receive during retirement and the taxation of investments. So we will conclude with this very important technique. It should be part of your repertoire if you have a legal or common-law spouse and if one of you is in a lower tax bracket than the other.

Splitting Retirement Income

Retirement income-splitting means transferring retirement income between you and your spouse or common-law partner in order to lower your overall taxes. The Canada Pension Plan may be split, but using the up to 50% of income that qualifies for the $2,000 pension income-tax credit that can be allocated to a spouse or common-law partner has far more potential.

Retirement income that is eligible for income splitting for people 65 and older includes: lifetime annuity payments under a registered pension plan; a registered retirement savings plan; a deferred profit savings plan; plus payments received from a registered retirement income fund. In other words, if you were receiving $50,000 per year from your RRIF, $25,000 could be transferred for tax purposes to your spouse.

For those younger than 65, lifetime annuity payments made through an RPP and certain death benefits are eligible for splitting.

Retirement income-splitting is beneficial in two ways. Firstly, it can reduce income tax if one of the spouses has higher retirement income and is in a higher marginal tax bracket than the other.

Secondly, retirement income-splitting is beneficial if you or your spouse are 65 or older and receiving OAS payments. As we have seen, OAS benefits are clawed back once a person's annual net income reaches $64,718 (in 2008) and completely clawed back when the net income reaches $104,903 (in 2008). If you split retirement income so that both of you are under the $64,718 threshold, you can each receive the maximum OAS benefit.

Income splitting can also be accomplished by:

- using the age of a younger spouse on a RRIF;
- increasing the investment base of the lower-income spouse;
- making a spousal loan to the lower-income spouse;
- making transfers for fair market value;
- making contributions to a spousal RRSP;
- assigning CPP income to the lower-income spouse.

ATTRIBUTION RULES

The attribution rules of the Canada Revenue Agency prevent a taxpayer from transferring, loaning, or gifting property to a spouse or close family member to avoid or reduce tax on that property. So, if a high-income earner made a loan to his or her spouse in a lower tax bracket, any income or loss from the property, including any capital gain or loss on the disposition of the property, must be reported by the higher-income earner. If the property is transferred at fair market value, attribution rules do not apply.

Use the Age of Younger Spouse on RRIF

If you do not need the income from your RRIF and have a spouse who is younger, withdrawals from your RRIF should be based on the age of your spouse. Less money will be withdrawn from the RRIF in the early years, leaving more money in the fund, longer.

Increasing Investment Base of Lower-Income Spouse

This may be accomplished by having the higher-income spouse pay the household expenses (rent, mortgage, utilities, groceries, credit-card bills, etc.), as well as the income-tax liability of the lower-income spouse.

This allows the lower-income spouse to maintain a larger investment base with which to earn future income, to be taxed at a lower rate, and to invest those funds that otherwise would be used to pay income taxes.

The higher-income spouse can pay the interest on an investment loan made by the lower-income spouse only when the loan is made by a third party. No income is attributed to the higher-income spouse, while the lower-income spouse may deduct those interest payments on the loan from his or her tax return.

Spousal Loans

Attribution rules do not apply when property or funds are loaned, provided that interest on the loan is charged at the CRA-prescribed rate, and paid.

Therefore, if assets are expected to produce a return well in excess of the minimum rate of interest charged, lending the assets or funds at an interest rate that avoids attribution effectively transfers the excess yield to the lower-income spouse.

Transfer for Fair Market Value (FMV)

Since attribution rules do not apply when property is transferred for consideration equal to its fair market value, such a transfer to the lower-income spouse may be beneficial when the assets transferred are expected to increase in value or produce a high yield in the future.

Contributions to Spousal RRSP

Tax rules allow for the high-income-earner to contribute to the RRSP of the lower-income-earning spouse (subject to the normal limits) and claim the tax deduction.

Since the recipient spouse will ultimately report the income for tax purposes when the funds are withdrawn, and if he or she has less income than the donor spouse, either on retirement or some time earlier, he or she may pay significantly less tax on that income.

To prevent immediate "income splitting," the amount contributed will be taxed back to the donor spouse to the extent of any amount withdrawn by the recipient spouse in the year in which it is contributed or in the next two calendar years.

For example: Sophia, who earns significantly more than Pablo, her artist spouse, contributes $7,000 to Pablo's RRSP in January 2002, and claims the tax deduction on her 2001 tax return. If Pablo withdraws the funds at any time up to the end of 2004, up to $7,000 of the amount withdrawn will be treated as Sophia's income, not Pablo's. Note, however, if Sophia had made the contribution in December 2001, Pablo need only wait until the end of 2003 before withdrawing the funds This difference of a year can be significant, because Pablo could lose a year of compounded interest if he chooses to invest the money.

Assigning CPP

As a strategy for tax saving through income splitting, the higher-income spouse can direct up to 50% of his or her CPP benefits to the lower-income-earning spouse.

This may be done, provided both spouses are over age 60. If this is done, a portion of the recipient spouse's CPP is automatically transferred back to the first spouse.

If the transferring spouse has high CPP benefits and the recipient spouse has low, or no, CPP benefits, the assignment can effectively transfer up to half of the CPP income to the lower-income spouse.

The amount that can be transferred, up to a maximum of 50%, depends on the length of time the spouses lived together as a proportion of their total contributory period.

For example: Lucy has a marginal tax rate (MTR) of 50% and her husband, Harold, has a MTR of 26%. Lucy's CPP benefit is $750 a month or $9,000 annually. Harold's CPP benefit is $250 a month or $3,000 annually. Before income splitting, the household tax bill would be:

Lucy, $4,500 ($9,000 x 50%)
Harold, $780 ($3,000 x 26%)
Total: $5,280

After splitting:

Both are now receiving $6,000 annually. ($12,000 ÷ 2)
Lucy now pays $3,000 in tax ($6,000 x 50%)
Harold now pays $1,560 in tax ($6,000 x 26%)
Total household tax bill is now $4,560 for an annual saving of $720.

Retirement Planning Worksheets

If you are using the retirement planning worksheets and are married, you might choose to develop two plans: one for you as an individual, if you cease to be married for any reason at or during retirement, and one for you as a married couple. You should not base your retirement plan on the assumption that you will be married, especially if (as is likely to be the case) this results in a lower savings rate. One partial solution is to use the insurance worksheet to cover the shortfall that will occur if your spouse dies, but this solution will not work if you are separated or divorced. The best solution is simply to plan for the worst-case scenario, i.e., the plan that requires the highest savings rate, to cover all eventualities.

We suggest you photocopy the following worksheets so you can work out changing scenarios.

HOW MUCH WILL MY CURRENT SAVINGS BE WORTH AT RETIREMENT?

This worksheet provides two methods of estimating the future value of your current savings based on **asset class** or **historical performance**, depending on whichever method is better suited for you (or a combination). Performance based on asset class is better where you are holding a portfolio of cash, bonds, stocks, etc., in which you know the asset allocation of each class. Historical performance is better if you are holding investment funds (e.g., mutual funds) with established long-term rates of return (at least ten years is recommended). You may use a combination of techniques, provided you do not include any asset more than once.

In order to use this worksheet you must know the current value of each category of asset that you expect to turn into cash in retirement (*do not include the value of any asset, e.g., a home, that you do not intend to convert into retirement income*), because different kinds of assets have different rates of return.

You must also decide on a rate of return and an inflation rate based on historical averages. For your information the historical lows, highs, and averages of inflation and different asset classes are given in the shaded tables to guide you. If you wish to be conservative, add a percent or two to the inflation rate and subtract a percent or two from the rates of return. Conversely, if you wish to create an optimistic forecast, subtract a percent or two from the inflation rate and add a percent to the rates of return. (*Historical lows and highs are included for informative purposes, as an indication of volatility, but don't use these numbers in your calculations.*) Also, if you are planning for the short term (say, five years), it might be better to choose a number close to the current actual rates rather than the historical averages, if they differ.

Simply subtract the inflation rate you choose from the rate of return you choose to arrive at an inflation adjusted rate of return, i.e., the real rate of return after allowing for the decay in purchasing power caused by inflation. Enter in your HP 10BII financial calculator the years to retirement, inflation adjusted rate of return, and current value to arrive at a future value in current dollars for each asset category, using the table entitled "Future Time Value of Money Calculation" at the end of the worksheet.

If you intend to sell your property at retirement, assume 2.5% appreciation for a rural property or 5% for an urban property, because these are the historical average rates of return for real estate. (On the worksheet, the real-estate total is net of commission)

The future value of your current savings is the sum of the future value in current dollars of all asset categories.

Note that the method presented in this worksheet decreases in accuracy with shorter time periods.

Disclaimer: The use of average rates of return provides a useful approximation, especially over the long term, but becomes less accurate over shorter time horizons due to the fluctuations of market cycles. For more accurate and reliable planning results, the use of a good retirement planning program is highly recommended.

Years to Retirement

This worksheet is for the _____ years from 20___ to 20___.

GUIDELINES ONLY, PROVIDED FOR INFORMATION PURPOSES

Historical Inflation Rate (Consumer Price Index), 1946–1999

Low	High	Average
–2.1%	18.1%	4.26%

Historical Rates of Return for Different Asset Classes, 1946–2007*

Asset Class	Historical Rates of Return		
	Lo	Hi	Av
Cash (T-Bills)	0.38%	15.49%	4.76%
Bonds	–8.25%	32.81%	5.83%
Stocks	–9.97%	52.56%	15.13%
Mortgage Backed Securities	–0.87%	14.95%	7.72%

*Mortgage-Backed Securities, 1992–2002

Method A: Asset Class Calculation (Cash, Bonds, Stocks, Real Estate)

Note: Use the Time Value of Money Calculation, on p. 112, for each asset class and sum.

Asset Class	Present Value	Inflation Adjusted Assumed Rate of Return Based on Historical Averages*		Future Value
		Actual	Your Assumed Rate	See Calculations p. 112
Cash		0.5%		
Bonds		1.5%		
Stocks		10.4%		
Mortgage-Backed Securities		3.3%		
TOTAL				

* Subtracting the inflation rate from the nominal rate of return provides a fair approximation of the real rate of return, which can also be calculated more accurately by dividing 1 + the nominal rate of return by 1 + the inflation rate. For example, for cash the simplified formula produces an estimated real rate of return of 4.76 – 4.26 = 0.5%. The more accurate formula is 1.0476 ÷ 1.0426 – 1 x 100 = 0.48%. The figures provided are based on the more accurate method. You may use these numbers or assume your own.

Method B: Historical Calculation (Mutual Funds)

Use the Time Value of Money Calculation, below, for each investment fund and sum.

Fund	Current Value	Long-Term Historical Net Average Rate of Return	Minus: Assumed Inflation Rate	Future Value in Current Dollars
TOTAL				

Summary

TOTAL PORTFOLIO (METHOD A)	
TOTAL INVESTMENT FUNDS (METHOD B)	
REAL ESTATE (AFTER COMMISSION)	
OTHER	
TOTAL FUTURE VALUE OF SAVINGS	

Future Value of Money Calculation (HP 10BII)

Repeat for each asset class or investment fund and sum.

Step	Key	Press	Display will show
1.	Years to retirement	N	
2.	Inflation adjusted rate of return	I	
3.	Current value, ±	PV	
4.	0	PMT	0
5.	**Future value?**	FV	

My current savings at retirement in current 20__ dollars will be worth: $__________

WHAT ARE MY RETIREMENT GOALS?

This is simply a rough worksheet, to get you thinking.

I would like to retire at age: _______

During my retirement years, I would like to: ______________

____

____

	Income	Expense	Net
☐ Buy or lease a car	$_______	$_______	$_______
☐ Become a landlord	$_______	$_______	$_______
☐ Buy or rent a cottage	$_______	$_______	$_______
☐ Buy insurance	$_______	$_______	$_______
☐ Buy real estate	$_______	$_______	$_______
☐ Contribute to charity	$_______	$_______	$_______
☐ Deplete my estate	$_______	$_______	$_______
☐ Dine out less	$_______	$_______	$_______
☐ Dine out more	$_______	$_______	$_______
☐ Get a pet	$_______	$_______	$_______
☐ Get a reverse mortgage	$_______	$_______	$_______
☐ Give gifts to others	$_______	$_______	$_______
☐ Go on a cruise	$_______	$_______	$_______
☐ Invest	$_______	$_______	$_______
☐ Join a club	$_______	$_______	$_______

☐ Leave an estate	$______	$______	$______
☐ Maintain my standard of living	$______	$______	$______
☐ Move	$______	$______	$______
☐ Open a trust fund	$______	$______	$______
☐ Pay down my debt	$______	$______	$______
☐ Pursue a hobby	$______	$______	$______
☐ Pursue leisure activities	$______	$______	$______
☐ Pursue sporting/ recreation activities	$______	$______	$______
☐ Read	$______	$______	$______
☐ Renovate/refurnish	$______	$______	$______
☐ Rent out	$______	$______	$______
☐ Sell my car	$______	$______	$______
☐ Sell my property	$______	$______	$______
☐ Shop	$______	$______	$______
☐ Start a business	$______	$______	$______
☐ Stay in my home	$______	$______	$______
☐ Take courses	$______	$______	$______
☐ Travel	$______	$______	$______
☐ Work full-time	$______	$______	$______
☐ Work part-time	$______	$______	$______
☐ Other	$______	$______	$______

Once you've identified your chosen retirement lifestyle, itemize, describe, and cost the items you've checked above, as well as any other special items not included in the list. For example, if you've checked Move, begin by writing a short description, on a separate piece of paper, of where you want to move, into what sort of accommodation, whether the move will yield any income (e.g., selling a home), and how much it will cost, including packing and transportation costs, acquisition or renting costs, etc. Once you've costed out all the items, use this information in the next worksheet along with your other expenses in order to estimate the gross income you will need to retire.

HOW MUCH WILL MY/OUR RETIREMENT EXPENSES AND REQUIRED INCOME BE?

For each income and expense item enter the item in the column corresponding to how it is normally received or spent (always move to the right). For every item calculate a Yearly amount by multiplying by the appropriate factor (daily = 365; weekly = 52; monthly = 12). Complete this worksheet in conjunction with the **What Are My Retirement Goals** worksheet. Estimate all expenses in current dollars. (*If you wish to make a comparison with your current budget, this worksheet can also double as an all-purpose budget/cash-flow planner.*)

This Worksheet Applies from Age _____ to Age _____

Retirement Cash Flow Statement (Projected)

	Daily	Weekly	Monthly	Yearly
Expenses				
HOUSEHOLD				
Cleaning				
Computer				
Condominium Fees				
Domestic Help				
Electricity				
Food				

	Daily	Weekly	Monthly	Yearly
Furnishings				
Garbage				
Garden Supplies				
Heat				
Insurance				
Maintenance and Repairs				
Mortgage				
Pets				
Property Taxes				
Renovations/ Improvements				
Rent				
Second Mortgage/ Home Equity Loan				
Security				
Supplies				
Water				
Other				

	Daily	Weekly	Monthly	Yearly
FAMILY				
Alimony and Child Support				
Child and Baby				
Childcare/ Daycare				
Education				
Other Dependent				
Other				
MEDICAL				
Dental				
Chiropractic				
Drugs				
Naturopathy				
Physiotherapy				
Other				
INSURANCE				
Additional Property/ Liability				
Critical Illness				

	Daily	Weekly	Monthly	Yearly
Disability				
Life				
Long-Term Care				
Medical/ Dental				
Other				
DEBT SERVICE				
Bills				
Credit Cards				
Personal Line of Credit				
Personal Loans Incurred to Earn Income				
Other Personal Loans				
RRSP Loans				
Student Loans				
Tax Assessments				
Other				

	Daily	Weekly	Monthly	Yearly
WORK-RELATED				
Business Income Expense				
Insurance				
Professional/ Union Dues				
Other				
TRANSPORTATION				
Car Insurance				
Car Lease				
Car Maintenance				
Car Purchase				
Fuel				
Parking				
Public Transit				
Taxi Fare				
Other				
COMMUNICATION				
Cell				

	Daily	Weekly	Monthly	Yearly
Internet				
Postage and Stationery				
Telephone				
VOIP				
Other				
EDUCATION				
Books and Supplies				
RESP				
Tuition				
Other				
TRAVEL				
Accommodations				
Air Fare				
Boat Fare				
Car Rental				
Food				
Public Transportation				

	Daily	Weekly	Monthly	Yearly
Taxi Fare				
Time Share/ Property Abroad				
Train Fare				
Other				
ENTERTAINMENT				
Alcohol				
Books/ Magazines/ Newspapers				
CDs/DVDs/ videos				
Eating Out/ Takeout/ Ordering In				
Hobbies				
Tobacco				
TV				
Other				
PERSONAL				
Clothing				

	Daily	Weekly	Monthly	Yearly
Grooming				
Health and Exercise Fees/ Equipment				
Laundry/Dry Cleaning				
Memberships				
Pocket Money				
Other				
GIFTS				
Charitable Contributions				
Personal Gifts				
Political Memberships/ Contributions				
Other				
PERSONAL SAVINGS				
Non-registered Savings				
Personal Property				
RPP				

	Daily	Weekly	Monthly	Yearly
RRSP				
Tax Free Savings Account				
Trading Fees and Commissions				
Other				
TOTAL				

Simplifed Income Tax Calculation

A note about future taxes: No one knows what the future may bring, and this is especially true of taxes. Trying to accurately estimate future taxes is an exercise in futility. The simplified method presented here is based on the Average Marginal Tax Rate for your income after deducting the Basic Personal Amount ($10,100 in 2009). This should result in a fair approximation.

Marginal Tax Rates

If your income is between $8,930 and $37,180, use a MTR of 24%.

If your income is between $37,180 and $74,360, use a MTR of 35%.

If your income is between $74,360 and $120,890, use a MTR of 42%.

If your income is above $120,890, use a MTR of 46%.

Retirement Income Goal Calculation

		Yearly
Total Expenses		
x 100 ÷ (100 – MTR)		
+ Basic Personal Amount	+ $10,100	
Retirement Income Goal		

Note: If your retirement income goal pushes you up into the next higher MTR, repeat the calculation for the higher MTR.

My Retirement Income Goal at retirement in current 20__ dollars is: $___________ (after taxes)

HOW MUCH CPP WILL I RECEIVE AT RETIREMENT?

Note: The rules governing CPP eligibility and benefits are complex. The following summarize the basic rules only. For more information concerning CPP, and to obtain an official estimate of your future CPP entitlement (recommended), visit http://www.hrsdc.gc.ca/en/isp/pub/factsheets/retire.shtml. The current CPP payment rates are posted at http://www.hrsdc.gc.ca/en/isp/pub/factsheets/rates.shtml.

Basic Eligibility Requirements

- ✔ I am 65 years old or older and
- ❑ I have made at least one valid contribution to the CPP

- ✔ I am between 60 and 65 years old
- ❑ I have made at least one valid contribution to the CPP
- ❑ I have stopped working or earn less than $884.58 during the month I will begin collecting CPP and the month previous.

A. CPP Entitlement Calculation

To determine your future CPP entitlement, you can contact the government, *or* make a list of every year that you have worked and earned income on which you paid CPP contributions since age 18 to the present, and estimate your approximate annual income for each year. Be as accurate as possible. If your average income is higher than $42,591.84, enter $10,614.96, since this is the maximum pension benefit for 2008. Strike out the 15% of years when your income was lowest, as well as any years when your income was low due to the raising of a child under seven years of age, provided at least ten years of earnings are left over. Of the years that are left over, calculate the average annual income and then multiply by 25%. If you know what your future income is likely to be, e.g., based on a known formula governing annual wage increases, and you expect to stay in the same job for the foreseeable future, include this in your calculation. Assuming you continue to work at his level at least until retirement, this will be close to your actual pension entitlement, up to the maximum of $10,614.96 (2008), assuming the rules governing eligibility or benefits don't change. Enter the result or $10,614.96, whichever is lower, to the right.

$__________ (A)

B. Adjustment for Early or Late Retirement

If retiring *before* 65:

65 – _____ (age at retirement) = __________ x 6%

$__________
(Maximum 30%)

If retiring *after* 65 (maximum is 70 years):

_____ (age at retirement) – 65 = __________ x 6%

$__________
(Maximum 30%)

$__________ (B)

Estimated CPP Benefit

$__________ (A + B)

HOW MUCH OAS WILL I RECEIVE AT RETIREMENT?

Note: The rules governing OAS eligibility are complex. The following summarizes the basic rules only. For more information concerning OAS, especially if you have any doubt concerning your possible ineligibility, visit http://www.hrsdc.gc.ca/en/isp/common/hrsdc/ris/risoas.shtml. OAS payment rates are posted here: http://www.hrsdc.gc.ca/en/isp/oas/oasrates.shtml

Basic Residency Requirements

✔ I live in Canada and

❑ I am a Canadian citizen or a legal resident of Canada

❑ I have lived in Canada for at least ten years since age 18

✔ I live outside Canada and

❑ I was a Canadian citizen or a legal resident of Canada when I left Canada

❑ I lived in Canada for at least 20 years since age 18

Short Residency Adjustment (short residency is less than 40 years)

40 – Number of years of residence in Canada up to 40 (if zero or negative go to to next step) __________

÷ 40 x $6069.96 = (A) $__________

OAS Clawback Adjustment

Retirement Income (use your retirement income goal from earlier worksheet)			$__________
			– $64,718
			__________
OAS Clawback	x 15%	(B)	$__________

Net OAS Calculation

Maximum OAS Entitlement (2008)	$ $6,069.96
Minus: Residency Adjustment	__________
Minus: OAS Clawback	__________
Net OAS	$__________

HOW MUCH MORE RETIREMENT INCOME WILL I NEED, IF ANY?

Summary of Retirement Income Sources

Include only retirement income sources that are known and established.

Income Source	Amount
CPP/QPP	$
OAS	$
DBP/Other Pension Plan(s)	$
Other Investment Fund(s)	$
Annuity(ies)	$
Trust Fund(s)	$
Rent	$
Work	$
Any Other Income	$
TOTAL RETIREMENT INCOME FROM ALL KNOWN SOURCES	$

Calculation of Retirement Income Shortfall/Excess

Income Source	Amount
Required Income Goal (from **How Much Will My/Our Retirement Expenses and Required Income Be?**)	$
Minus: Total Retirement Income from All Sources	$
REQUIRED CAPITAL INCOME (copy into **How Much in Savings Will I Need to Retire**) (if negative number, enter zero)	$

My retirement income shortfall/excess in 20__ dollars is: $__________

HOW LONG SHOULD I PLAN FOR?

	Male				Female			
Your Age Now	Your Probability of Survival to Age ______							
	40%	30%	20%	10%	40%	30%	20%	10%
20-45	81	84	87	91	87	89	92	96
50	81	84	87	91	87	90	92	96
55	82	84	87	91	87	90	92	96
60	82	85	88	91	87	90	93	96
65	83	85	88	92	88	90	93	96
70	84	86	89	92	88	91	93	96

Source: Statistics Canada

For many people leaving an estate is not realistic, whereas future rates of return on annuities are uncertain. If this applies to you, your best option might be to time your retirement savings to gradually deplete till the end of life. For those who make this choice and, to a lesser extent, also for those who must anticipate their post-retirement spending in a retirement budget, which may change over time, a mandatory component of the time value of money calculation is N—i.e., the number of years remaining till the end of life. Failure to tackle this question realistically raises the spectre of outliving one's money, which can result in impoverishment or worse at the very end of life, when one is most vulnerable. With the doubling of medical knowledge every ten years, many people are living longer. Many people grossly underestimate their life expectancy. Statistical averages are also misleading, since 50% of the population will outlive their statistical average life expectancy for at least some period of time.

The best single predictor of longevity is one's current age. The table above shows the life expectancy of 40%, 30%, 20% and 10% of the Canadian population between the ages of 20 and 70. The reliability of a retirement plan will inversely correlate with the probability of survival, and should certainly not be less than 70%, i.e., the 30% survival column. If one uses this column for planning there is a 1 in 3 probability of outliving one's money for at least some period of time. The 20% to 10% survival columns, corresponding to 80% and 90% reliability respectively, represent higher degrees of certainty. A 100% reliable plan will of course assume the genetically maximum life expectancy of 115 to 120 years, but will also be significantly more expensive.

To use the mortality calculator above for planning purposes, find your current age and gender and try to design your personal financial plan around one of the ages in the shaded area for 80% to 90% reliability, unless you have strong specific reasons to think that these statistical averages may not apply to you. If in doubt, you should also discuss the matter with your doctor.

HOW MUCH LIFE INSURANCE DO I NEED?

1. If I were to die today, what immediate expenses would be incurred? *(Note: Only include one-time liabilities that will be paid off immediately, and revise this calculation regularly.)*

Education fund	
Emergency fund	
Funeral and burial/cremation expense	
Pay off car loan	
Pay off debt/taxes	
Pay off mortgage	
Probate, legal and administrative fees (est.)	
Transitional expenses for survivor	
(A) TOTAL CASH NEEDED AT DEATH	

2. In the event of my death, what liquid assets will be immediately available? *(Note: Only include assets of the estate that will be received or liquidated at or shortly after death, after deducting any commissions, taxes, or other associated expenses.)*

Cash or near-cash (e.g., T-bills, CSBs, etc.)	
Death benefits – CPP/QPP	
Death benefits – RPP	
Investment portfolio	
Life insurance – group	
Life insurance – personal	
Real estate	
RRSP assets	
Any other assets to be liquidated	
(B) TOTAL LIQUID ASSETS AT DEATH	

How much extra cash will be required at death? (A – B)

(C) ______________

3. In the event of my death, how much extra long-term income will be required by my survivor(s) (*if any*)?

	PER MONTH	PER YEAR
Lost income/required income (e.g., 70–80% of current income)		
(MINUS: Survivor's benefits)		
(MINUS: Childrens' benefits)		
NET ADDITIONAL INCOME REQUIRED		
(DIVIDED BY: Assumed Rate of Return on Capital, e.g., 4% or 5%)		

TOTAL ADDITIONAL CAPITAL REQUIRED

(D) ______________

(Note: This calculation assumes indefinite continuation of the required nominal income. The capital needed may be reduced by assuming a limited term and depletion to zero over the course of the term. This calculation requires the use of a financial calculator. The assumed rate of return on capital may or may not be adjusted for inflation.)

TOTAL LIFE INSURANCE REQUIRED (C + D)
(if result is negative, no more insurance is needed)

____

HOW MUCH IN SAVINGS WILL I NEED TO RETIRE?

1. What is your capital income requirement after deducting all other sources of income (CPP, OAS, other pension plans, working, insurance, etc.) based on other worksheets?

CAPITAL INCOME REQUIREMENT	$

2. Choose your basic retirement plan:

Plan A. Leave an estate. This can be your net worth at retirement or some other amount, either less or more. Plan A enables you to leave an estate for your survivors.

Plan B. Deplete estate to nothing. This possibly risky strategy requires you to estimate your life expectancy in retirement. You control the degree of risk by increasing or decreasing your life expectancy assumption (e.g., an assumed life expectancy of 120 is devoid of risk, because the maximum human life span is 115 to 120 years, barring a major medical breakthrough). See the **How Long Should I Plan For?** worksheet. Plan B allows you to continue to manage your own money, possibly at a higher rate of return than an annuity, without leaving an estate.

Plan C. Buy an annuity. Different types of annuities with many different payout options and conditions are available. The highest rate of return is a single life annuity, which will pay out a specified income for life with no risk of outliving your money (both indexed and non-indexed options are available). Annuity rates have however been dropping over the past couple of decades (see below). The disadvantage of an annuity is that, if you buy into one when the market is down, you can never undo your decision.

Future rates of return are inherently unpredictable and therefore difficult to plan around. You can also combine your choices, purchasing an annuity with some of your capital and investing the balance.

A word about indexing. Unless you have strong reasons to believe that your mortality will be sooner rather than later, indexing your retirement is strongly recommended. Say you retire at age 65 and inflation averages 4% per year. Say your health takes a turn for the worse at age 75 and you find your cost of living increases suddenly. If your income is not indexed, the purchasing power of your income at age 75 will be only 66% of what it was when you retired. The only situation in which indexing might be able to be ignored is if your initial retirement income is very generous.

Plan A. Leave an estate.

4% Rule Method

The widely recommended 4% rule of thumb simply indicates the amount of money that you can withdraw from your investment fund without depleting your capital. It assumes that you withdraw 4% of your capital in the first year of retirement, and then increase that amount by the inflation rate in each subsequent year. Thus, your retirement income is indexed.

Required Income*	÷	.04	=	Required Capital
$				$

* This amount can be increased every year by the current rate of inflation.

Time Value of Money Method

Use your HP 10BII financial calculator to produce a more individualized result.

Step	Key	Press	Display will show
1.	Assumed years of retirement	N	
2.	Inflation adjusted rate of return	I	
3.	Capital income requirement	PMT	
4.	Desired value of estate at N, ±	FV	
5.	**Required capital?**	PV	

Plan B. Deplete estate to nothing.

Plan B uses the same time-value-of-money calculation as above, by entering zero as the FV. This alternative incurs the risk of outliving one's money. Therefore the value input for N must be carefully considered. It is better to err on the high side than outlive your money.

Step	Key	Press	Display will show
1.	Assumed years of retirement (120 – retirement age is essentially risk free)	N	
2.	Inflation adjusted rate of return	I	
3.	Capital income requirement	PMT	
4.	0	FV	
5.	**Required capital?**	PV	

Plan C. Buy an annuity

The basic annuity calculation is similar to the 4% rule of thumb presented above, except that you have to assume what the future rate of return of an annuity will be, establishing the purchase price of the annuity. The annuity itself has little risk, but there is risk in predicting what the rate of return of an annuity might be in the future. For this reason it is important to be conservative.

Required Income		Assumed Annuity Rate of Return		Required Capital
$	÷		=	$

The following chart shows the historical rates of return of annuities between 1984 and 1999. As you can see, annuity rates have been dropping steadily since 1990 and are now (2008) about 7%.

Annuity Rates of Return, 1984-1999

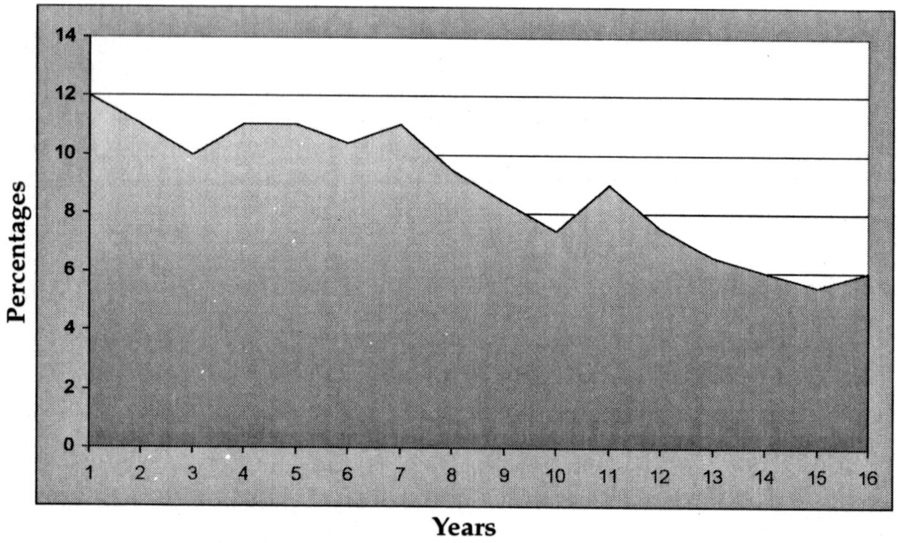

HOW MUCH DO I NEED TO START SAVING NOW?

This worksheet provides two methods of estimating the rate of return of your projected savings based on **asset class** or **historical performance**, depending on whichever method is better for you (or a combination). Performance based on asset class is best where you are holding a portfolio of cash, bonds, stocks, etc., in which the asset allocation of each class is accurately known. Historical performance is better if you are holding investment funds with established long-term rates of return (at least ten years is recommended). You may use a combination of techniques, provided you do not include any asset more than once.

In order to use this worksheet you must know the percentage in your portfolio of each category of asset that you expect to realize in retirement (*do not include any asset, e.g., a home, that you do not intend to convert into retirement income*). You must also estimate an assumed rate of return and an assumed inflation rate based on historical averages. Simply subtract the assumed inflation rate from the assumed rate of return to arrive at an inflation-adjusted rate of return. Then, enter the years to retirement, inflation-adjusted rate of return, current savings, and required capital in your HP 10BII financial calculator to arrive at the annual savings required to reach your retirement capital objective within the specified time horizon.

If you do intend to sell your property at retirement, assume 2.5% appreciation for a rural property, 5% for an urban property.

If you wish to be conservative, add a percent or two to the inflation rate and subtract a percent or two from the rates of return. Conversely, if you wish to create an optimistic forecast, subtract a percent or two from the inflation rate and add a percent to the rates of return. (*Historical lows and highs are included for informative purposes but don't use these numbers in your calculations.*) Also, if you are planning for the short term (say, five years), it might be better to choose a number close to the current actual rates rather than the historical averages, if they differ.

Note that the required savings must be incremented each year by the actual inflation rate.

Note that the method presented in this worksheet decreases in accuracy with shorter time periods.

Disclaimer: The use of average rates of return provides a useful approximation, especially over the long term, but becomes less accurate over shorter time horizons due to the fluctuations of market cycles. For more accurate and reliable planning results, the use of a good retirement planning program is highly recommended.

Years to Retirement

This worksheet is for the _____ years from 20___ to 20___.

GUIDELINES ONLY, PROVIDED FOR INFORMATION PURPOSES

Historical Inflation Rate (Consumer Price Index), 1946–1999

Low	High	Average
–2.1%	18.1%	4.26%

Historical Rates of Return for Different Asset Classes, 1946–2007*

Asset Class	Historical Rates of Return		
	Lo	Hi	Av
Cash (T-Bills)	0.38%	15.49%	4.76%
Bonds	–8.25%	32.81%	5.83%
Stocks	–9.97%	52.56%	15.13%
Mortgage-Backed Securities	–0.87%	14.95%	7.72%

* Mortgage-Backed Securities, 1992–2002

Method A: Asset Class Calculation (Cash, Bonds, Stocks, Real Estate)

Multiply the Percentage of Portfolio by the Rate of Return to arrive at the Rate of Return adjusted for the percentage of the portfolio, eg., 10% x 5% = 0.5%. The overall portfolio rate of return is the sum of the result for each asset class.

Asset Class	Percentage of Portfolio	Inflation Adjusted Assumed Rate of Return Based on Historical Averages*		Assumed Rate of Return Adjusted for Percentage of Portfolio
		Actual	Your Assumed Rate	
Cash		0.5%		
Bonds		1.5%		
Stocks		10.4%		
Mortgage-Backed Securities		3.3%		
TOTAL				

* Subtracting the inflation rate from the nominal rate of return provides a fair approximation of the real rate of return, which can also be calculated more accurately by dividing 1 + the nominal rate of return by 1 + the inflation rate. For example, for cash the simplified formula produces an estimated real rate of return of 4.76 – 4.26 = 0.5%. The more accurate formula is 1.0476 ÷ 1.0426 – 1 x 100 = 0.48%. The figures provided are based on the more accurate method. You may use these numbers or assume your own.

Method B: Historical Calculation (Mutual Funds)

Fund	Current Value	Long-Term Historical Net Average Rate of Return	Minus: Assumed Inflation Rate	Future Value in Current Dollars
TOTAL				

Summary

TOTAL PORTFOLIO (METHOD A)	
TOTAL INVESTMENT FUNDS (METHOD B)	
AVERAGE ESTIMATED OVERALL RATE OF RETURN	

Time Value of Money Calculation (HP 10BII)

Step	Key	Press	Display will show
1.	Years to retirement	N	
2.	Inflation adjusted rate of return	I	
3.	Current value, ±	PV	
4.	Required capital	PMT	
5.	**Required savings?**	FV	

I must save $__________ in current 20__ dollars each year.

MY RETIREMENT PLAN: SUMMARY OF RESULTS

Fundamental Retirement Planning Assumptions

Current Date	
Current Age	
Retirement Age (Worksheet 2)	
Years to Retirement	
Maximum Longevity Assumption (Worksheet 7)	
Retirement Plan (Worksheet 9)	☐ Leave an estate ☐ Deplete estate to % ☐ Buy an annuity
Indexation of Retirement Income (recommended)	☐ Yes ☐ No

Summary of Results from Worksheets

	From Worksheet	Current Dollars
Current Retirement Assets (Net Worth)	1	$
Future Value of Current Savings at Retirement	1	$
Projected Retirement Expenses	3	$
Estimated Retirement Taxes	3	$
Retirement Income Goal	3	$
Estimated CPP Income	4	$
Estimated OAS Income	5	$
All Other Retirement Income (Estimated)	6	$
Total Projected Retirement Income from All Known Sources	6	$
Retirement Income Shortfall	6	$
Required Life Insurance	8	$
Required Total Savings at Retirement	9	$
Annual Savings Goal	10	$

Glossary

The Financial Literacy You Need for Retirement Planning

To understand the subject you need to know the lingo. These are the terms you should know in order to communicate effectively with your banker:

Assets

Everything a company or a person owns or has owed to it.

Assignment (CPP)

If you have contributed to CPP, and both you and your spouse or common-law partner are at least 60 years old, you can share your CPP pension. This is called an assignment.

The assignment of CPP redistributes income from one person to another; the amount of pension is not increased or decreased by assignment. The benefit of doing so is to move income to the spouse who is in a lower tax bracket and thus pay less tax on what you receive. An assignment will end if you divorce, if your non-contributor spouse becomes a contributor, if either you or your spouse die, or one year after you separate.

Attribution rule

A Canada Revenue Agency rule that states that an investor cannot avoid paying taxes at their marginal rate by transferring assets to other family members who have lower personal tax rates.

Average monthly pensionable earnings

Your *average monthly pensionable earnings* (AMPE) are used to determine the amount of your monthly retirement pension. It is your total pensionable earnings divided by the number of months that you contributed (or 120 months, whichever is greater). Your monthly retirement pension at age 65 is 25% of the AMPE to a maximum. The maximum CPP pension in 2008 was $884.58.

Another way to look at this is:

a) Determine Total Pensionable Earnings:
All pensionable earnings together = total pensionable earnings

b) Determine Average Monthly Pensionable Earnings
The greater of:

$$\frac{\text{Total Pensionable Earnings}}{\text{No. of Months of Contributions or 120 months (whichever is greater)}} = \text{Average Monthly Pensionable Earnings}$$

Bond

A certificate evidencing a debt on which the issuer promises to pay the holder (or buyer of the bond) a specified amount of interest based on the coupon rate for a specified length of time, and to repay the loan on its maturity date.

Bridge benefits

Some plans will pay you a bridge benefit from retirement until the age when your government pensions begin. The benefit may be a flat dollar amount or it may be tied to CPP and/or OAS benefits. The amount of benefit will be shown on your pension statement if it is provided by the pension plan.

For example, Josh retires from his company when he is 61 years old. He doesn't want to receive his CPP until he turns 65, and his benefit amount will be $650 a month. His company pension plan will pay him $650 a month on top of his regular pension until he starts receiving his CPP.

Call options

The right to buy a specific number of shares at a specified price (known as the strike price) by a fixed date. The buyer pays a premium to the seller of the call option. An investor would buy a call option if the price of the underlying stock is expected to rise.

Canada Pension Plan/Quebec Pension Plan

The Canada Pension Plan (CPP) is a mandatory contributory pension plan designed to provide monthly retirement, disability, and survivor benefits for all Canadians. Employers and employees make equal contributions. Quebec has its own parallel pension plan, the Quebec Pension Plan (QPP).

Cash surrender value

In an insurance policy, it is the amount of cash that has accumulated in the insurance policy and may be withdrawn by the insured. The cash value can be accessed as a lump sum, or it can be annuitized. Annuitization converts the cash value into an annuity.

When you take the cash value, you surrender the policy, which is where the name cash *surrender value* came from. Whether you take the money or convert the policy to an annuity, there will be a taxable gain that you must declare as income in the year you receive the funds.

You calculate the taxable gain by taking the adjusted cost basis for the policy—basically how much was paid in premiums—and subtracting from that the cost of your life insurance coverage (your company can tell you this net cost of pure insurance, known as NCPI). You then subtract this sum from the cash surrender value and the taxable gain is the amount that remains.

Clawback

This is the term in the Income Tax Act (ITA) that requires Canadians with higher incomes to repay all or part of any social benefits, such as Old Age Security payments, that they receive in any year. If you continue to work after the normal retirement age, you may find that your income reduces your OAS benefits, and in fact, all those who earn more than $64,718 in 2008 will start to see their OAS benefits reduced. Those with a net income of $104,903 in 2008 are subject to a full clawback, in which all their OAS benefits must be repaid to the federal government.

Common shares

Securities, usually representing ownership in a company. These shares carry voting privileges and are entitled to the receipt of dividends, if dividends are declared by the board of directors.

Commuted value

If you leave a company, and were in its defined-benefit pension plan, your vested benefits—the Commuted Value of the defined-benefit plan—can be transferred to a locked-in plan, such as a locked-in Registered Retirement Savings Plan or another registered pension plan, or can be used to purchase an annuity. The Commuted Value, or Transfer Value, is a lump-sum payment. The basis for calculating the value is dictated by the Canadian Institute of Actuaries.

Cost of living adjustment (COLA)

About 20% of the defined-benefit plans in Canada provide for an automatic cost of living adjustment (COLA). If the COLA is automatic, the statement will inform you how the adjustment is to be applied. Without a COLA, over your retirement you will see a loss of purchasing power that results from creeping inflation.

Some COLAs do not apply unless the Consumer Price Index exceeds a certain minimum level, such as 3%. Alternatively, your employer may increase pensions at irregular intervals when the company feels the purchasing power of the pensions has been eroded. These are called ad hoc increases. Your pension statement will be silent on this point, because it is not guaranteed.

Deferred life annuity

This is a type of contract sold by life insurance companies, which pays a regular stream of income to the beneficiary or annuitant at some agreed-upon starting date in the future. The original payment is either a lump sum or a stream of payments made over time, ending prior to the beginning of the annuity payments. You might choose this because you'll get more money when the annuity begins or because you need more time to pay into the annuity.

Deferred profit-sharing plan (DPSPs)

These are trusts registered with Revenue Canada. An employer makes cash contributions to the plan from business profits for those employees who are members of the plan.

The contributions and earnings accumulate in the plan tax-free. All DPSPs must provide for employee vesting. A DPSP does not allow any of the beneficiaries of the plan to be related to a shareholder who owns more than 10% of the voting shares of the company. Only the employer makes contributions.

Defined-benefit plan (DBP)

This is a type of registered pension plan where the formula which determines the pension benefit at retirement is known, whereas the contributions needed to fund the benefit are not. There is no investment risk to the employee with a DBP. The retirement benefit does not depend on market performance.

Defined-contribution pension plan (DCP)

This is a type of registered pension plan where the amount contributed is known but the dollar amount of the pension is unknown. The pension amount depends on the investment results. This plan is also known as a money purchase plan (MPP).

Equity mutual funds

An investment fund operated by a company that uses the proceeds from shares and units sold to investors to invest mainly in stocks. (Part of the fund can be held in cash or money-market securities to be used for redemptions, held for investment opportunities, or held back from investing in stocks if the money manager's outlook for stocks is not favourable). One of the keys to long-term accumulation of wealth rests with stocks or equity mutual funds. All professional money managers agree that you must have a percentage of your investment asset mix in stocks/equities in order to counter the effects of inflation. In fact, many financial analysts believe the rule of thumb for the best asset mix for wealth accumulation is that the amount in bonds should equal your age, and the balance should be in equities.

Fair market value

This is the price an asset or property would sell for in the marketplace. When you are doing a net worth statement, you will list your assets at their fair market value. Stop-loss rules exist to prevent people who are not dealing at arm's-length from deferring tax on gains by transferring property for an amount that is below the property's fair market value.

Future value of money

This is the amount that a dollar today will be worth at some point in the future. For example, $100 today will be worth $134.39 in ten years time if it is invested and earns 3% compounded annually. (*See also* **Inflation**)

Group retirement savings plans (GRSPs)

Group retirement savings plans provide benefits similar to those offered by individual RRSPs, except your employer, union, or professional association administers them on a group basis. Your contribution by wage deduction is matched wholly or partially by the employer, union, or association. All employer contributions are a taxable benefit to you.

On retirement, a GRSP allows you to choose a life annuity, a registered retirement income fund (RRIF), a cash payment, or a combination of these options.

Like Deferred Profit-sharing Plans, Group Retirement Savings Plans are not "locked in" and can be cashed in whenever you decide, depending on the terms of the plan.

Guaranteed Income Supplement (GIS)

Old Age Security recipients who have no other, or low, incomes will qualify to receive the guaranteed income supplement. You must be 65 or older and pass an annual income test.

You cannot plan to receive the GIS; you will receive it only as an emergency measure that will top you up to where you would be if you lived on welfare payments.

The GIS is paid differently for single pensioners and for married pensioners. The amount a single pensioner receives is reduced by $1 for each $2 of other monthly income; the amount a married pensioner receives is reduced by $1 for each $4 of the couple's other combined monthly incomes. More details on GIS rates and the Allowance (see below) can be acquired from Human Resources and Skills Development Canada.

You must reapply annually for the GIS. Benefits are not taxed and will continue to be paid if you leave Canada for up to a maximum of six months.

Guaranteed Investment Certificates (GICs)

A deposit instrument most commonly available from trust companies, requiring a minimum investment at a predetermined rate of interest for a stated term. GICs are a popular investment choice because they are easy to buy, their principal and interest are guaranteed, and they offer a variety of terms and rates. Further, you can use them as collateral for a loan, and they are automatically renewed at maturity.

GICs are available in both redeemable and non-redeemable forms; the non-redeemable GIC cannot be cashed before maturity, except in the case of death or extreme hardship.

Two disadvantages associated with GICs is that they are not all RRSP eligible and they are not covered by the Canada Deposit Insurance Corporation if their term is longer than five years. The interest earned in a GIC is taxable as income.

Income splitting

A tax-planning strategy whereby the higher-earning spouse transfers income to the lower-earning spouse or common-law partner to reduce taxable income. The Canada Pension Plan may be split. However, there is much more potential in using the up to 50% of income that qualifies for the $2,000 pension income-tax credit that you can allocate to a spouse or common-law partner.

Retirement income that is eligible for income splitting for people 65 and older includes: lifetime annuity payments under a registered pension plan; a registered retirement savings plan; a deferred profit-sharing plan; plus payments received from a registered retirement income fund. In other words, if you were receiving $50,000 per year from your RRIF, $25,000 could be transferred for tax purposes to your spouse.

Income trusts

A type of investment trust that holds investments in the operating assets of a company. Income trusts are similar to closed-end mutual funds in that you purchase an ownership interest in the trust and all revenue and expenses of the trust flow through to you. In the past, trusts distributed their earnings to investors, who, in turn, paid taxes on the income. New regulations introduced in 2006 leave trusts with less to give out to investors. Most income trusts do not trade over the counter or on an exchange.

Since trust expenses are usually higher than income earned in the early years of the trust, these trusts are often used as a tax-deferral strategy for higher-income investors.

The trusts hold properties (e.g., real estate) or assets (e.g., oil and gas projects) to produce income.

They are somewhat similar to bonds, because of the income they produce, but there are no guaranteed payouts.

Indexing

1. A portfolio management style that involves buying and holding a portfolio of securities that matches closely or exactly the composition of a benchmark index (such as the S&P/TSX Composite Index).

2. Having a stream of income such as an annuity payment that increases each year to keep up with inflation.

Individual pension plans (IPPs)

A registered defined-benefit pension plan set up for one person that specifies the level of payments to the plan holder. It is most suitable for those who are 40 or older and earn an annual salary (T4 income) of more than $100,000 (approximately).

IPPs were designed with business owners in mind. They provide a tax advantage to the member, because contributions are tax-free, and a tax advantage to the business, because the contributions, set-up, and administrative costs are tax-deductible expenses. When a company borrows funds to make contributions, interest payments are also tax deductible.

The initial contribution to the plan can cover all the unused RRSP contribution room of the IPP member dating back to the incorporation of the firm.

There are two types of IPP:

1. A Shareholder Pension Plan for owner/managers who own more than 10% of the shares of the company.
2. An Executive Pension Plan for new shareholders or those who own less than 10% of the shares of a company. These are often used as an executive perk to attract or retain senior management.

Inflation

A generalized, sustained trend of rising prices. For instance, if you need $40,000 worth of income to cover living expenses when you retire, and inflation is averaging 2% per year, you will need almost $49,000 per year to pay the same expenses in only ten years' time. In 20 years, a 2% inflation rate means you will need close to $60,000.

On the other hand, $40,000 in earning power today will be worth only $32,877 in five years' time at an annual inflation rate of 4%.

Inflation Rate

The rate of change in prices. The Consumer Price Index (CPI) is the index that measures the cost of living by measuring the prices of a given basket of goods. It is the indicator of inflation. For example: if the CPI for this year was 152 and the previous year it was 148, what was this year's rate of inflation?

Rate of Inflation = [(current year's CPI – previous year's CPI) ÷ previous year's CPI] x 100
Rate of Inflation = [(152 –148 = 4) ÷ 148] x 100 = 2.7%

Insured annuity

An insured annuity is essentially a prescribed life annuity (see **prescribed life annuity**) and a term-to-100 life insurance policy, purchased together. The combination of the benefits provided by these products is ideal for you if you are seeking guaranteed income and the preservation of your capital. Term-to-100 life insurance is a permanent policy that will be in force until you die. It is the least expensive form of permanent insurance.

Laddering

An example of laddering is to buy GICs or bonds so that 20% of the total matures every year, and not at the same time (thus reducing risk and providing some liquidity). Then the maturing principal is reinvested each year for a new five-year term. By doing this, you may benefit from any future increase in interest rates, and you will have the option to reinvest at current interest rates. Laddering ensures flexibility and a steady income. (It is also called staggering maturities.)

Leveraged deferred compensation plan (LDCP)

The Leveraged Deferred Compensation Plan combines the benefits of a universal life insurance policy with a loan to provide an income in retirement. The LDCP is a way to grow a tax-sheltered investment; it allows clients to tap into the value of a life insurance policy tax-free while they are still alive. It does not allow the payment of tax-free benefits until after death.

Example of How the LDCP works:

Firstly, if you are seeking to use the LDCP, you take out a universal-life insurance policy. Universal-life insurance is comprised of term life insurance with a savings or investment fund that is sheltered from tax. Then, on retirement, you use the investment value of the policy as collateral for a loan from a financial institution. The financial institution advances payments to you free of tax. Interest on the loan is charged at the going rate (e.g., prime + ?% to 1%), and it can be accumulated or paid yearly. As interest accumulates, the amount of the loan increases, while the value of the life insurance to the estate decreases.

Finally, on your death, the policy proceeds are used to pay the loan plus interest; the remaining value of the policy is paid out tax-free to the policy beneficiaries.

Life annuity (or Straight Life Annuity)

An immediate annuity that pays the purchaser a guaranteed monthly or annual income until he or she dies. This provides the highest amount of guaranteed income per dollar of annuity premium paid (i.e., when the annuitant dies, the payments stop, and a residual payment is not made to the annuitant's estate or beneficiaries). The annuity payments are made up of blended capital and income. An advantage of a straight life annuity is that the annuitant cannot outlive his or her capital.

Life Income Fund (LIF)

These are purchased with locked-in retirement savings from plans such as locked-in retirement accounts (LIRAs), locked-in pension funds, or locked-in RRSPs. LIFs offer a flexible retirement income option; the principal and income remain tax sheltered until withdrawn, and there is a range of investment options to choose from, similar to those held within an RRSP or LIRA. The owner of the LIF controls the amount of income (within limits) that he or she will receive, and income payments must begin no later than the end of the year after the LIF is opened. LIFs are also referred to as Locked-in RRIFs.

LIRA (Locked-in Retirement Account)

This was previously known as a locked-in RRSP. The LIRA is established with the institution of choice. Because it is locked-in, the funds can be withdrawn only for retirement purposes.

Locked-in RRSP

Now known as a LIRA. Because it is locked-in, the funds can be withdrawn only for retirement purposes. LIRAs must be used to purchase a life annuity or a LIF.

LRIF (Locked-in RRIF)

These are either called a LIF or a LRIF, depending on which province you are in. While a RRIF can be opened at any age, a LIF owner must be at least 55 years of age. The earliest date that funds can be transferred to a LIF depends on the province in which the client's pension benefits are deemed to have been earned.

Income-stream options from a LIF are similar to a RRIF, in that the plan holder must withdraw a minimum amount each year; a LIF is unlike a RRIF, in that there is a maximum amount that can be withdrawn. The maximum is determined by a formula that applies a term-certain annuity to age 90 to the value of the fund at the beginning of each year. This limit prevents the plan holder from cashing out the plan (unlike a RRIF, which may be cashed out at any time).

Managed plans

RRSPs in which your deposit is invested in products held in trust under the plan. No further investment decisions are required by you.

Marginal tax rate (MTR)

The tax rate that would have to be paid on any additional dollars of taxable income you earned.

Market value adjustment (MVA)

A market value adjustment is basically a penalty that reflects any changes in the interest rate between the time an annuity contract was taken out and the time it is being surrendered. It is used when there is an early surrender or partial withdrawal of an annuity contract. This information should be sought from the company that holds the annuity for you.

Mortgage-backed securities (MBSs)

This is an investment vehicle that allows an investor to share in the cash flow from a portfolio of residential mortgages. The pool of home mortgages is insured under the National Housing Act (i.e., the federal act that oversees the approved mortgage insurers in Canada). Units of a MBS pay interest and a part of principal each month and, if homeowners prepay their mortgages, may pay out additional amounts of principal before normal maturity. They trade in the bond market at prices reflecting current interest rates.

Mutual funds

An investment fund operated by a company that uses the proceeds from shares and units sold to investors to invest mainly in stocks, bonds, derivatives, and other financial securities. Mutual funds offer investors the advantages of diversification and professional management. They are sold on a load (commission or sales charge) or no-load basis. The share/units are redeemable on demand at the fund's current net asset value per share (NAVPS). Mutual funds are widely available through insurance-company subsidiaries, banks, and investment dealers.

Net worth

A snapshot at any point in time which totals up the market value of all assets you own and subtracts all the outstanding debts that you owe. The remaining sum is your net worth.

Old Age Security (OAS)

Old Age Security is a monthly benefit payable to all Canadians or legal residents age 65 or over who meet residence requirements. It is funded from general tax revenues, and the benefits, which are tied to increases in the CPI, are adjusted quarterly. Benefits received from the OAS are taxable income.

Payouts

The amount of payments from a pension plan or withdrawals from a RRIF or similar plans are called payouts.

Pensionable earnings

This is the sum of earnings from employment or self-employment which is used to determine the contribution amounts for CPP/QPP contributions.

Preferred shares

A class of share capital that entitles the owners to a fixed dividend ahead of the company's common shares and to a stated dollar value per share in the event of liquidation. They usually do not have voting rights unless a stated number of dividends have not been paid.

Prescribed annuity

Provides a level after-tax income by spreading the tax load over the life of the annuity.

A non-prescribed annuity contract pays more interest in the early years of the contract and more capital later.

Present value of an annuity

This is how much needs to be saved to yield a specific income received at the beginning of the year or the end of the year.

Real-estate investment trusts (REITs)

An investment trust that specializes in real-estate-related investments, including commercial mortgages, construction loans, land and real-estate securities in varying combinations. Investors buy units in the trust. REITs enable small investors to make investments in commercial real estate that would not normally be available to them.

Registered pension plan (RPP)

A trust registered with Canada Revenue Agency (CRA) and established by an employer to provide pension benefits for employees when they retire. Both employer and employee may contribute to the plan, and contributions are tax-deductible. (See **DBPs** and **DCPs**).

Retirement compensation arrangement (RCA)

Like Individual Pension Plans, Retirement Compensation Arrangements are used by:

- owners of privately held corporations;
- corporate executives making more than $85,000 annually;
- people who might retire outside Canada.

An RCA is established by an employer as a taxable trust. The trust holds the funds for retirement. Contributions to an RCA are split 50/50 between the trust account and a refundable tax account held by Canada Revenue Agency. The funds that go into the refundable tax account are not invested and are simply returned in the same amounts as they were contributed.

Retirement goal

A retirement goal is simply an idea of what you want to do—for instance, retire at age 60. A retirement goal leads to a retirement objective.

Retirement objective

The objective is the amount of money you need to turn the goal into reality, let's say $500,000.

Reverse mortgage

A reverse mortgage is a type of loan that is used to convert the equity in a home into cash. Retirees who find themselves cash poor and house rich can use the money obtained through a reverse mortgage to achieve financial security at the expense of their estate value. The amount advanced under the mortgage (up to 50% of the home value) depends on the value of your home, your age, and your marital status. The proceeds may be taken as a lump sum, as guaranteed monthly payments, or as a combination of the two. Essentially, a reverse mortgage is the reverse of a conventional mortgage. Instead of you paying the lender each month, the lender pays you.

Rights

A short-term privilege granted to a company's common shareholders to purchase additional common shares, usually at a discount from the market price, from the company itself. There is a stated price and they must be purchased within a stated time period. Rights of listed companies trade on stock exchanges from the ex-rights date (i.e., two business days before the date on which the shareholder officially owns the shares) until the expiry date.

RRIF (Registered Retirement Income Fund)

A tax-deferral vehicle available to RRSP holders. This is the most popular maturity option of RRSP holders. The RRIF must be established by the end of the year the RRSP holder turns 71 years of age. The process for conversion is simple: the proper forms are signed and the RRSP funds are transferred into the RRIF account. Other types of deposits cannot be made to a RRIF.

You keep control of your RRIF funds; you also retain some of the same flexibility that existed in the RRSP.

An annuity can be purchased with RRIF money, but a RRIF cannot be funded from an annuity.

The RRIF pays out regular and gradually increasing payments until it is exhausted (at about the time you reach age 94).

Self-directed plans

A type of RRSP whereby the holder invests funds or contributes certain acceptable assets, such as securities, directly into the RRSP. A bank, trust company, or investment dealer administers your assets for a fee. You make all investment decisions.

Spousal trust

You would receive income from a spousal trust if your spouse created the trust during his or her lifetime, though it would not be until he or she died that assets would flow into the trust for your benefit.

If you are the sole beneficiary, assets transfer to the trust tax-free. The assets are considered the capital of the trust; the income created by those assets will form the income you receive from the trust. You must receive all of the income of the trust during your lifetime; no other person may obtain or use the income or capital of the trust while you live.

Spousal trusts are used to take advantage of tax savings and to protect the estate assets in the event that the surviving spouse remarries.

Stocks (same as common shares)

Securities usually represent ownership in a company, and these shares carry voting privileges and are entitled to the receipt of dividends, if dividends are declared by the board of directors.

Straight life annuity (same as a life annuity)

An immediate annuity that pays the purchaser a guaranteed monthly or annual income until he or she dies. This provides the highest amount of guaranteed income per dollar of annuity premium paid (when the annuitant dies, the payments stop and a residual payment is not made to the annuitant's estate or beneficiaries). The annuity payments are blended capital and income. An advantage of a straight life annuity is that the annuitant cannot outlive his or her capital.

Stripped bonds (or zero-coupon bonds)

Usually high-quality federal or provincial government bonds, originally issued in bearer form (i.e., no registered owner). Some or all of the interest coupons have been detached. The bond principal (the residue) then trades separately from the detached coupons, which can also trade separately from the principal. They trade at discounts from their maturity values. The gain received from the purchase price and the maturity value is taxed as investment income.

Supplemental executive retirement plan (SERPs)

A supplemental executive retirement plan is a pension plan that is established for people whose benefits have reached the tax limits of a registered plan. There is no limit on benefits of a SERP. SERPs see highly paid executives earning the same percentage of their income in their pension as lower-paid workers, because they get around a government cap in pension payouts that affects those earning more than $100,000 per year. That cap means that those earning $500,000 would receive the same pension payout as those earning $100,000.

Tax-free savings account (TFSA)

This is not law yet. It was introduced in the February 2008 budget. Essentially it says that, starting in 2009, Canadians will be able to invest up to $5,000 a year in a TFSA. Contributions will not be tax deductible, but growth through capital gains, interest, and dividends will not be taxed, even when withdrawn. After withdrawals, the amounts can be replenished with no tax consequences.

Term-certain annuity

A term-certain annuity, pays you a guaranteed income for either:

- a defined period of time (e.g., 5 years);
- a period ending at a specified age, e.g., age 85, at which time the annuity matures; or
- a specified period, equal to the number of years from your age at purchase to age 90, or until your spouse turns 90.

A term-certain annuity can be bought with either a single premium (a lump sum) or a series of premiums over a period of time. If you die before the term is completed, the income is paid to your beneficiary, either for the balance of the term, as a lump sum, or to your estate.

It is also known as an ***annuity certain*** or a ***fixed-term annuity***.

The Allowance

A pensioner's spouse between the age of 60 to 65, who meets the OAS residence requirements and also meets an income test, is eligible for a monthly allowance. The maximum spouse's allowance is the sum of the OAS pension plus the guaranteed income supplement (GIS) pension, at the married rate.

Time value of money

This is how much an investment, paying compound interest, will be worth at the end of a period of time.

Transfer value (same as commuted value)

If you leave a company and were in its defined-benefit pension plan, your vested benefits, the Commuted Value of the defined-benefit plan, can be transferred to a locked-in plan, such as a locked-in Registered Retirement Savings Plan or another registered pension plan, or can be used to purchase an annuity. The Commuted Value, or Transfer Value, is a lump-sum payment. The basis for calculating the value is dictated by the Canadian Institute of Actuaries.

Transitional retirement

Transitional, or phased, retirement is a relatively new concept that acknowledges that a person may not be psychologically prepared to move from the full-blown work environment to the full-blown non-work environment. It is a way to ease into retirement that can begin when you are satisfied that you can afford to retire and your employer is prepared to have you work less than the regular work week.

Treasury bills (T-bills)

Short-term government debt issued in denominations ranging from $1,000 to $1,000,000. T-bills do not pay interest but are sold at a discount and mature at par (i.e., 100% of face value). The difference between the purchase price and par is the purchaser's income in lieu of interest. In Canada, this gain is taxed as interest income.

Variable annuity

This guarantees a fixed number of monthly unit payments. The value of the unit payments varies according to the value of the investments in a special "segregated" fund (usually made up of acceptable common stocks) into which premiums are placed. Many variable contracts provide a "floor" below which benefits may not fall.

Vested benefit

Vesting is the employee's right to an employer's contribution made to the employee's pension plan. The amount is the vested benefit. If you terminate your employment before you are vested, you are entitled to only your contributions with interest, up to the termination date of employment. The minimum period in which vesting can occur is two years.

Warrants

A certificate giving the holder the right to purchase securities at a stated price within a stated time period. Warrants are usually issued with a new issue of securities as an inducement or sweetener to buy the new issue.

Year's basic exemption (YBE)

This is the level of income that can be earned in order to make participation in either the CPP/QPP compulsory. Most Canadian workers between the ages of 16 to 65, as well as self-employed persons who earn more than YBE (currently at $3,500), must contribute to the CPP/QPP.

Year's maximum pensionable earnings (YMPE)

This is the amount of earnings from employment or self-employment which is used to determine the contribution amounts for CPP/QPP contributions.

If you are earning more than the YMPE, you are not allowed to make additional contributions above the maximum limit. Any excess contributions are refunded.

CPP contributions kick in after you have earned $3,500 (the YBE). Conversely, CPP contributions are not made on amounts you earn over $44,900 (in 2008). This is called the *year's maximum pensionable earnings* (YMPE).

It is the amount between this minimum and maximum on which your contribution is based; this is called your pensionable earnings. Therefore, if you earn more than $44,900, your pensionable earnings will be $41,400 ($44,900 – $3,500). But if you earned, let's say, $30,000 your pensionable earnings would be $26,500 ($30,000 – $3,500).

Index

ORDER FORM

Please send me:

_____ copy/copies of Estate Planning, Life Insurance and Taxes for Canadians @ $19.95/copy $________

_____ copy/copies of Retirement Planning and Taxes for Canadians @ $19.95/copy $________

_____ copy/copies of Investing for Retirement and Taxes for Canadians @ $19.95/copy $________

Subtotal	$________
GST @ 5%	$________
Shipping and handling	$________
Total price	$________

Special Pricing: Order any two books @$34.95 or $49.95 for all three (plus GST and $5.95 shipping and handling)

Method of Payment:

❑ cheque enclosed (made payable to Oliver Publishing)

❑ credit card:

❑ VISA

❑ Mastercard

❑ American Express

Number on card: ______________________________

Expiry date: ________ / ________ /

Shipping Address:

Name: ______________________________

Address 1: ______________________________

Address 2: ______________________________

City/Town: ______________________________

Province: ______________________________

Postal code: ______________________________

❑ Is this a gift? Name on gift enclosure:

To: ______________________________

From: ______________________________

Message: ______________________________

____

Send to:

Oliver Publishing, 151 Bloor Street West, Suite 800, Toronto, ON M5S 1S4